Muy Bueno

FIESTAS

The secret ingredient
is always love

Muy Bueno

FIESTAS

100+ DELICIOUS MEXICAN RECIPES
FOR CELEBRATING THE YEAR

Yvette Marquez-Sharpnack

Photography by Jenna Sparks

weldon**owen**

Contents

8 Introduction

LENT

15 Roasting Chile Peppers
16 Chilaquiles Divorciadas
18 Red & Green Chile Cheese Enchiladas
20 Beer-Battered Shrimp Tacos
23 Sopa de Chacales
24 Spinach & Bean Tacos
27 Veracruz-Style Tilapia
28 Mar y Tierra Molcajete
30 Tres Leches Bread Pudding with Bourbon Sauce
32 CRAFT: Clothespin Cross

VALENTINE'S DAY

39 Cheese Board
40 Heart-Shaped Berry Empanadas
43 Cajeta Thumbprint Cookies
45 Dulce de Leche Brownies
46 Chocolate Mousse
49 Mexican Chocolate Martini
50 Passion Fruit Margarita

SAINT PATRICK'S DAY

57 Mexican Beef & Guinness Stew
58 Corned Beef Brisket Tacos
61 Pipián Verde
62 Irish Soda Bread with Roasted Green Chile
64 Mexican Chocolate Stout Cake with Irish Whiskey Ganache
67 Café de Olla with Irish Liqueur

EASTER

73 Barbacoa de Borrego
74 Ham & Sweet Potato Hash
77 Ensalada de Coditos
78 Spring Fruit Salad with Tajín
80 Mango & Strawberry Galette
82 Mini Empanadas with Apricot-Jalapeño Jam & Cream Cheese
84 Mexican Sprinkle Cookies
87 Bloody María with Serrano-Infused Tequila
88 CRAFT: Cascarones

CINCO DE MAYO

95 Tequila & Lime Carne Asada
96 Cochinita Pibil with Spicy Pickled Onions
99 Lamb Birria
102 Guacamole with Pomegranate
105 Jalapeño Mandarin Margarita
106 Baked Churros with Lavender-Lemon Buttercream
108 CRAFT: Papel Picado

MOTHER'S DAY

114 Mexican Coffee Cake
117 Caballeros Pobres
118 Gorditas de Picadillo
121 Huevos Rancheros
122 Tampiqueña Steak
125 Fresh Fruit Cups with Chamoy & Tajín
126 Guava Mimosas
128 CRAFT: Paper Flowers

FATHER'S DAY

135 Machaca con Huevo
136 Gringa al Pastor
141 Sopaipillas Stuffed with Beef & Beans
143 Grilled Pineapple Smoked Mezcal
145 Crispy Pork Carnitas
146 Michelada & Chelada

FOURTH OF JULY

153 Mexican Beer Queso Dip

154 Hatch Chile Potato Salad

157 Beer Brats with Onions, Bell Peppers & Roasted Green Chile

158 Ranchero Burgers

160 Steak Fajitas

161 Chiles en Escabeche

162 Elote

165 Salsa de Molcajete

166 Sandía con Agua Mineral

MEXICAN INDEPENDENCE DAY

173 Lime Corn Tortilla Chips

174 Flautas de Carne Deshebrada a la Bandera

177 Chiles en Nogada

180 Strawberry & Pistachio Paletas

183 Agua de Tamarindo

184 Tequila Tasting Party

HALLOWEEN

191 Spicy Roasted Pepitas

192 Chile Colorado con Carne y Papas

194 Slow-Cooker Pot Roast

195 Calabaza en Tacha

197 Witches' Fingers Sugar Cookies

198 El Ojo

DÍA DE LOS MUERTOS

205 Day of the Dead Altar

206 Spinach & Chile Verde Tortillas

208 Sopa de Verduras

211 Chile Braised Pork Ribs

212 Camotes Enmielados

215 Pan de Muerto

217 Horchata & Mexican Chocolate Conchas

220 Marranitos (Pig-Shaped Cookies)

222 Atole

225 Blood Orange Marigold Margarita

226 CRAFT: Sugar Skulls

THANKSGIVING

232 Bolillos

235 Chipotle Mashed Sweet Potatoes

236 Rajas con Queso

238 Chorizo & Bacon Stuffing

240 Pavo Enchilado

242 Empanadas de Camote

244 Mexican Sangria

247 Torta & Taco Bar with Thanksgiving Leftovers

CHRISTMAS, NEW YEAR'S EVE, AND EPIPHANY

253 Ensalada de Nochebuena

254 Turkey Pozole Verde

256 Orange Biscochos

258 Red, White & Green Polvorones

260 Buñuelos with Gingerbread Pilonchillo Syrup

262 Rosca de Navidad

265 Poinsettia Punch

266 Tamalada

270 Red Chile & Chicken Tamales

274 Sweet Raisin Tamales

277 Mexican Hot Chocolate

278 CRAFT: Tamal-Shaped Christmas Ornaments

FAMILY FIESTAS

285 Arroz Blanco Mexicano

286 Sopa de Letras

289 Mole Rojo

290 Polvorones

293 Watermelon-Pineapple Tequila Punch

294 Acknowledgments

297 Index

Introduction

Growing up, a fiesta meant countertops laden with potluck foods, cousins playing hide-and-seek, adults playing poker and drinking Tecate, and grabbing a plate of food to eat whenever you were hungry. It also offered the aroma of plump tamales and *frijoles de la olla* slowly cooking on the stove top. No matter what the occasion, we shared laughs and stories to the beat of Spanish music from a record player. Those lively get-togethers that once seemed to stretch endlessly now seem to fly by faster with each passing year.

Food will always be my way of keeping traditions alive and honoring Mexican culture, but I've realized that it serves another equally important function for my family: *slowing down time*. Serving a special dish has the power to ease even the busiest of moments, whether you're in the middle of a workweek or entertaining family-style for a holiday.

Unfortunately, that ease often only comes when you have trusted voices to guide you. Without the helpful hints from your mother or *abuelita*, that sense of calm can quickly disappear. If a suggestion to make your *salsa de molcajete* in advance or to put your empanadas in the oven so guests smell them baking when they arrive is left out of the conversation, before you know it, you're flustered and still in your bathrobe with curlers in your hair when the doorbell rings. Or worse yet, you find yourself trapped in the kitchen all evening preparing dishes at the last minute while your guests are enjoying the party.

As someone who was raised in a family that places enormous value on food, I have learned that cooking Mexican cuisine takes practice and a plan. But I also know that life is too short to worry about what you're cooking.

I have written *Muy Bueno: FIESTAS* to take the worry out of hosting fiestas and to help you find that ease as you explore Mexican cuisine and adopt new traditions. Organized into fourteen chapters by fiesta, this book will inspire you throughout a year of celebrating American and Mexican holidays *con gusto*. You'll learn how to prepare classic recipes and reinvented favorites, such as Lamb Birria, Turkey Pozole Verde, and strawberry and mango galette drizzled with orange liqueur–spiked *dulce de leche*— dishes that challenge both the notion that Mexican food is just tacos and enchiladas and that cooking needs to be complicated.

The fiesta is the heart of the Mexican community, and food is the heart of the fiesta.

I have included freezer tips, alternative cooking methods, hacks for leftovers, and easy ingredient substitutions, and many recipes are designed so you can either make them for a small gathering or scale them up for a large fiesta. Whether you choose to produce an entire menu for a specific occasion or select just a single course to try, you will be able to enjoy Mexican food without the stress!

The following pages are filled with a tapestry of flavors from my travels to Mexico and from my hometown of El Paso, Texas, where I was inspired by my maternal grandma, who emigrated from Chihuahua. Whether you're making corned beef tacos with cabbage slaw for your Saint Patrick's Day fiesta, shaking up a batch of jalapeño-spiked mandarin margaritas for Cinco de Mayo, or baking Pan de Muerto for Día de los Muertos, you will be sampling some of Mexico's rich culinary history. Mixed in among the recipes are a handful of fun and festive traditional Mexican crafts, including *cascarones*, sugar skulls, and *papel picado*, that kids—and adults—will enjoy making.

Old-world Spanish proverbs and sayings are sprinkled throughout this book, but there is one that my grandmother (a matriarch who always had food on the stove, in the Crock-Pot, and spread across her table) said that best describes the beauty of cooking food that has a a backbone of tradition: *Panza llena, corazón contento* (Full stomach, happy heart).

I am sharing modern recipes as well as recipes that have been a tradition in my family for generations—recipes that are just too good to be kept secret. My wish is that you make these cherished dishes your very own because that is when time stretches and happy hearts and memories truly take hold.

LENT

Ash Wednesday marks the beginning of *Cuaresma*, or Lent, the forty-day fasting period (excluding Sundays) that precedes Easter and ends on Holy Saturday. On Ash Wednesday and on all Fridays during Lent, observant Catholics abstain from eating meat, though we do eat seafood. When I was growing up, Fridays meant meatless meals even when it wasn't the Lenten season. Every Friday, we all gathered at my maternal grandma's house for her famous chile and cheese enchiladas.

Although our family has not committed to the practice year-round, we still forego meat on Fridays during Lent. If you do observe Lent, remember, you don't have to give up *sabor* during this time of reflection, as this chapter illustrates. In addition to my grandma's chile and cheese enchiladas, I have included her version of the comforting and rustic northern Mexican soup known as *sopa de chacales* and her healthy and budget-friendly tacos filled with spinach and beans. I didn't grow up eating fish and shellfish other than canned tuna, but two of my favorite seafood dishes, fish prepared Veracruz-style and shrimp tacos, are ideal Lenten suppers. Here, too, you'll find a delicious fusion of two classic Mexican desserts, *capirotada* (bread pudding) and the rich three-milks mixture known as *tres leches*.

Although the Lenten season is most closely associated with giving up things that you enjoy, in *nuestra familia*, we prefer to spend our forty days focusing on what we do have: a happy and healthy family, a cozy *casa*, and a table that is always full of *comida y amor*. What more could we ask for?

But my mom constantly reminds me that Lent is a time of spiritual discipline, self-examination, and moderation as well. Fortunately, Lent lacks the distractions of Valentine's Day with all its sweets, Saint Patrick's Day with its corned beef and beer, or even Easter Sunday with its colorful eggs and chocolate bunnies, allowing more time to reflect on its deeper meaning.

One year my mom made crosses out of clothespins to commemorate the Lenten season, and I honored this new tradition by hanging one in my home. I have included the directions on how to make these clothespin crosses, and I encourage you to get kids involved in this craft project, as it offers a good opportunity to talk about why and how Lent is celebrated.

As you can see, abstinence might be on the menu during Lent, but deprivation definitely isn't. Even If you do not celebrate *Cuaresma*, I hope you will try some of my family's traditional Lenten dishes as well as some of my new pescatarian favorites.

Clockwise from top left: Creamy Green Chile
Sauce (page 18) / Red Chile Sauce (page 17) /
Roasted Tomatillo Salsa (page 17)

ROASTING
Chile Peppers

Chiles are at the heart of Mexican cuisine, and knowing how to roast them properly regardless of your kitchen setup is important. One of the scents that reminds me most vividly of my childhood is the warm, smoky aroma of roasted chiles, which my grandma frequently made for her salsa casera (homemade salsa). When I smell chiles roasting and hear them popping and hissing, it is as if I can see my grandma cooking in her kitchen again. Although she roasted chiles on a comal (cast-iron griddle), and my mom roasts chiles under the broiler, I love to stock up my freezer with fire-roasted Hatch and Pueblo chiles or buy fresh, and roast them directly over the open flame of a gas burner on my stove top. The flavor is about the same no matter which method you choose, so here I will use the broiler, as nearly every cook has one. Any fresh peppers, from Anaheim and poblanos to jalapeños, can be roasted according to these directions.

Preheat the broiler. Line a sheet pan with aluminum foil. Select firm, meaty chiles free of wrinkled skin. Rinse them thoroughly to remove any dust particles, pat them dry, and then pierce each chile with a knife. Arrange the chiles, generously spaced, on the prepared pan.

Place the pan under the broiler and broil the chiles, watching them closely and turning them as needed, until evenly blistered and mostly blackened on all sides, 3–5 minutes on each side. Transfer the chiles to a plastic bag and close the bag, or place them in a bowl and cover the bowl with plastic wrap, then allow them to steam for about 5 minutes.

Remove the chiles from the bag or bowl and peel off the blistered and charred skin. Then, using your fingers, carefully tear open each chile lengthwise, pull out and discard the seeds and the stem, and cut as directed in individual recipes. If preparing the chiles whole for stuffing (chiles rellenos), using a knife tip, cut a slit from about ½ inch (12 mm) below the stem end to within ¼–½ inch (6–12 mm) of the tip of each chile, gently pull the slit open, and remove and discard the seeds.

COOK'S NOTE: To roast chiles (or peppers) on a comal like my grandma did, heat the comal over medium-high heat on the stove top, then place the chiles on the hot surface. You will smell and hear the chiles begin to char before you see it happening. Once dark spots begin to appear on the underside, use tongs to turn the chiles every few minutes until they are evenly blackened and blistered on all sides. To roast chiles directly over the flame of a gas stove, turn on the heat to medium, place a chile directly on the burner grate, and listen for popping and hissing, which should take about 1 minute. Then, using tongs, turn the chile to char it on all sides. The method for roasting on a charcoal or gas grill is similar to the open-flame stove-top method, though the timing will vary depending on the intensity of the fire. Chiles roasted by any of these methods are then steamed, peeled, seeded, and stemmed the same way as for the broiler method. Peeled and roasted chiles can be stored in an airtight container in the refrigerator for up to a few days or in the freezer for up to 6 months, then thawed in the refrigerator before using.

CHILAQUILES
Divorciadas

Every Friday growing up, we had red enchiladas for dinner. And if there happened to be leftover sauce, I would always hope my grandma would make *chilaquiles rojos* for breakfast the next day. My grandma used to lightly fry the tortillas to make the chilaquiles a bit soggy, but I like my tortillas fried a bit longer so the chilaquiles are crunchier when they are served.

This recipe calls for both a red (*rojo*) sauce and a green (*verde*) salsa. In New Mexico, a dish that includes both sauces is called "Christmas," but in Mexico, it is called *divorciada* (divorced). It's the perfect solution when you simply can't decide between red or green. The Red Chile Sauce and Roasted Tomatillo Sauce in this recipe are staples of the Mexican kitchen and are used throughout this book.

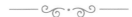

MAKES 2 SERVINGS

¼ cup (60 ml) canola oil

8 corn tortillas, cut into quarters

1 cup (240 ml) Red Chile Sauce, warmed (recipe follows)

1 cup (240 ml) Roasted Tomatillo Salsa, warmed (recipe follows)

½ cup (60 g) shredded Oaxaca or asadero cheese

⅓ cup (35 g) chopped green onions, white and pale green parts, or (50 g) red onion

2 large eggs, cooked any style (optional)

¼ cup (30 g) crumbled Cotija or queso fresco

Mexican crema, for serving (optional)

Fresh cilantro leaves, for garnish (optional)

Line a plate with paper towels and set it near the stove. In a large frying pan over medium heat, warm the oil. Add a single layer of tortilla quarters at a time and fry, turning as needed, until lightly browned and slightly crunchy, about 1 minute on each side. Transfer the tortilla quarters to the towel-lined plate to drain. Repeat with the remaining tortilla quarters.

Divide the fried tortillas evenly between 2 dinner plates. Drizzle ½ cup (120 ml) warm chile sauce over half of the tortillas on each plate and ½ cup (120 ml) warm tomatillo salsa over the other half on each plate. Sprinkle with the Oaxaca cheese and the onions, dividing them evenly, then top each serving with an egg, if using, and the Cotija cheese. Drizzle with the crema (if using), garnish with the cilantro (if using), and serve.

COOK'S NOTE: If you prefer a creamy green sauce, use Creamy Green Chile Sauce (page 18) or Pipián Verde (page 61) in place of the tomatillo salsa. Feel free to add carnitas (page 145), use sour cream in place of crema, or add other favorite toppings.

Red Chile Sauce

MAKES 3–4 CUPS (700–950 ML)

¼ lb (115 g) dried California or New Mexico red chiles

3 cups (700 ml) water

3 tablespoons all-purpose flour

2 cloves garlic, coarsely chopped

1½ teaspoons salt

Olive oil, for cooking

Remove the stems, seeds, and veins from the chiles, then put into a colander and rinse well under cool running water.

In a saucepan over high heat, combine the chiles with water to cover and bring to a boil. Reduce the heat to medium, cover, and simmer for 10 minutes. Using tongs, turn the chiles over so they will soften evenly, re-cover, and continue to simmer until softened, about 10 minutes longer. Drain well, discarding the water, and let cool for several minutes before blending.

In a blender, combine the cooled chiles, water, flour, garlic, and salt and purée until smooth. Pass the sauce through a fine-mesh sieve set over a bowl to remove the skins and seeds. Discard the solids in the sieve.

Use immediately, or transfer to an airtight container and store in the refrigerator for up to 1 week or in the freezer for up to 6 months.

To use the sauce, in a frying pan over medium heat, warm the oil, using 1½ teaspoons oil for every 1 cup (240 ml) sauce. Working carefully to avoid splatters, pour in the sauce and heat, stirring occasionally, until hot. Taste and adjust the seasoning with salt if needed.

Roasted Tomatillo Salsa

MAKES ABOUT 4 CUPS (950 ML)

1 lb (450 g) tomatillos (about 8 large), husked and rinsed

1 white onion, quartered

4 cloves garlic, unpeeled

2 serrano chiles, stemmed

Handful of fresh cilantro leaves

1 cup (240 ml) unsalted vegetable or chicken broth

2 tablespoons all-purpose flour

⅛ teaspoon salt

1 tablespoon olive oil

Position an oven rack about 4 inches (10 cm) from the heat source and preheat the broiler. Line a large sheet pan with aluminum foil.

Place the tomatillos, onion, garlic, and serranos on the prepared sheet pan, slip under the broiler, and broil the vegetables until blackened in spots on the top, about 6 minutes. Remove the garlic from the pan and flip the tomatillos, onion, and serranos. Return the pan to the broiler and broil until blackened in spots on the second side, 4–5 minutes. Remove from the broiler and let cool for several minutes before blending.

Peel the garlic cloves and add them to a blender along with the roasted tomatillos, onion, and chiles and the cilantro, broth, flour, and salt. Purée until smooth, then taste and adjust the seasoning with salt if needed.

In a large frying pan over medium heat, warm the oil. Working carefully to avoid splatters, pour in the blended sauce and bring it to a boil. Reduce the heat to a gentle simmer and simmer, stirring occasionally, until thickened, 6–8 minutes. Remove from the heat. Use immediately, or let cool, transfer to an airtight container, and refrigerate for up to 1 week or freeze for up to 6 months.

RED & GREEN CHILE
Cheese Enchiladas

"Red or green?" That's New Mexico's official question. Restaurants regularly give customers a choice of red chile sauce or green chile sauce on enchiladas, chiles rellenos, and other dishes. Opt for both and you have ordered your dish Christmas style. In New Mexico, cooks most commonly use dried New Mexico red chiles to make red chile sauce and Hatch green chiles to make green chile sauce. In Mexico, enchiladas topped with creamy green chile sauce are called *enchiladas suizas*. I grew up eating enchiladas topped with either red sauce or creamy green sauce. Combining the two sauces on one plate, as I have done here, is a match made in heaven.

MAKES 4 SERVINGS

CREAMY GREEN CHILE SAUCE

6 fresh Anaheim chiles, roasted, peeled, and seeded (page 15)

1 tablespoon all-purpose flour

1½ cups (350 ml) buttermilk

½ cup (115 g) sour cream or (120 ml) Mexican crema, plus more if needed

½ cup (120 ml) water, if needed

Salt

ENCHILADAS

1 tablespoon olive oil

2 cups (475 ml) Red Chile Sauce (page 17)

2 cups (475 ml) Creamy Green Chile Sauce

Canola oil, for frying

12–16 corn tortillas, preferably white corn

To make the green sauce, in a blender, combine the chiles, flour, buttermilk, and sour cream and blend until creamy. Pour the sauce into a frying pan, set over medium-low heat, and heat, stirring occasionally, until hot. The sauce should be pourable. If it is too thick, add as much of the water as needed to achieve a good consistency. If the sauce is too spicy, stir in additional sour cream as needed to temper the heat. Season to taste with salt. You should have about 4 cups (950 ml) sauce. Set aside 2 cups (475 ml) for the enchiladas. Let the remaining sauce cool, then store in an airtight container in the refrigerator for up to 5 days.

To make the enchiladas, first ready the sauces. In a frying pan over medium-low heat, warm the oil. Working carefully to avoid splatters, pour in the red sauce and heat, stirring occasionally, until hot. Taste and adjust the seasoning with salt if needed. In a second frying pan over medium-low heat, heat the green sauce, stirring occasionally, until hot. Keep both sauces warm while you assemble the enchiladas.

Line a plate with paper towels and set it near the stove. Pour the canola oil to a depth of ½ inch (12 mm) into a frying pan and heat over medium heat. When the oil is hot, slip a tortilla into the oil and fry, turning once with tongs, just until softened, about 30 seconds on each side. Transfer to the towel-lined plate to drain. Repeat with the remaining tortillas, stacking them as you go, keeping them warm, and adding more oil to the pan as needed.

2 cups (225 g) shredded white cheese, such as Oaxaca, Muenster, asadero, or Monterey jack, plus more for topping (optional)

1 white onion, finely diced

Mexican crema or sour cream, for topping

Fresh cilantro leaves, for garnish

Top each tortilla with an equal amount of the cheese and as much onion as you like, then roll up as tightly as possible and place seam side down on a large platter or on individual plates. Ladle the warm red sauce onto the enchiladas, covering just half of each enchilada. Then ladled on the warm green sauce, covering the other half of each enchilada. Top with additional shredded cheese, if desired, then garnish with the crema and cilantro and serve.

COOK'S NOTES: For a milder green sauce, substitute poblano chiles for the Anaheim chiles. For a non-creamy green sauce, substitute Roasted Tomatillo Salsa (page 17) for the green sauce. For mole enchiladas, substitute Pipián Verde (page 61) for the green sauce and Mole Rojo (page 289) for the red sauce.

These enchiladas can easily be made for a crowd. Preheat the oven to 350°F (180°C). Coat half of the bottom of a 9 x 13-inch (23 x 33-cm) baking dish with ½ cup (120 ml) of the red sauce, spreading it lengthwise. Then coat the other half of the bottom with ½ cup (120 ml) of the green sauce. Fill and roll the tortillas as directed and place them seam side down in a single layer on top of the sauces. Starting on the side of the dish coated with the red sauce, pour the remaining red sauce on top of the enchiladas, covering just half of each enchilada, then cover the other half of each enchilada with the remaining green sauce. Top with additional cheese, tent loosely with aluminum foil, and bake until the cheese is bubbly and the tortillas are lightly golden brown, 15–20 minutes.

BEER-BATTERED *Shrimp Tacos*

I love Baja-style fish tacos. This recipe is inspired by that tradition of light and flaky beer-battered strips of white fish tucked inside corn tortillas, but it calls for large shrimp in place of the fish. What's not to love?

MAKE 16 TACOS; 8 SERVINGS

SHRIMP

2 lb (1 kg) large shrimp, peeled and deveined

Salt

1 cup (125 g) all-purpose flour, plus more for dusting

1 teaspoon chili powder

½ teaspoon ground black pepper

¼ teaspoon dried Mexican oregano

1 cup (240 ml) dark Mexican beer

1 large egg

Vegetable oil, for deep-frying

CHIPOTLE CREAM SAUCE

1 cup (240 ml) Mexican crema or (225 g) sour cream

1 chipotle chile in adobo sauce, plus 1 tablespoon adobo sauce

1 teaspoon grated lemon zest

¼ cup (30 ml) fresh lemon juice

½ teaspoon kosher salt

16 corn tortillas, warmed

Avocado slices, fresh cilantro leaves, jalapeño slices, pickled onion slices, shredded red cabbage, salsa of choice, and lime wedges, for serving

To make the shrimp, pat them dry with paper towels, then put them into a bowl, season generously with salt, dust lightly with flour, and toss to coat evenly.

In a large bowl, combine the flour, chili powder, 1 teaspoon salt, the pepper, and the oregano and stir to mix. In a medium bowl, whisk together the beer and egg until blended. Pour the beer mixture into the flour mixture and whisk together lightly until no lumps remain. Set the batter aside to rest at room temperature while you prepare the sauce and heat the oil for frying.

To make the cream sauce, in a blender, combine the crema, chipotle chile and adobo sauce, lemon zest and juice, and salt and blend until smooth and creamy. If the sauce seems too thick, adjust with a little more lemon juice or with water. Cover and refrigerate until ready to use.

Have ready the tortillas and toppings.

To fry the shrimp, line a large plate with paper towels and set it near the stove. Pour the oil to a depth of about 1 inch (2.5 cm) into a large, deep frying pan and heat over medium-high heat to 350°F (180°C) on a deep-frying thermometer. Working in batches to avoid crowding, dip the shrimp into the batter, coating well and allowing the excess to drip off, then add to the hot oil. Fry the shrimp, flipping them once to ensure they cook evenly, until crisp and golden brown, about 2 minutes on each side. Using tongs or a slotted spoon, transfer to the towel-lined plate to drain. Repeat until all the shrimp are fried.

To assemble the tacos, place the shrimp on the tortillas, then top with the avocado, cilantro, jalapeño, onion, and cabbage. Drizzle with the cream sauce, then fold in half and serve with the salsa and lime wedges. Alternatively, invite your guests to assemble their own tacos. Serve at once.

Después de un buen taco, un bueno tabaco

Échale más agua al caldo

SOPA
de Chacales

Le ponemos más agua al caldo, or "we add more water to the broth," is a phrase popularly used by fiesta hosts. It means if someone wants to bring an extra guest along to a party, no worries. The cook will just add more water to the soup. This recipe, which is for a very old-world Mexican dish that you are unlikely to find on a restaurant menu, adapts well to an expanding party guest list. It is similar in flavor to *pozole rojo,* with *chacales,* dried and split corn kernels, replacing the hominy, but its cooking time is a bit longer. *Chacales* are sold in Latin markets, usually only during the Lenten season, though nowadays you can find them online as well.

———— ⟳·⟲ ————

MAKES 6 SERVINGS

1 bag (12 oz/340 g) chacales (about 2 cups)

13 cups (3 l) water

1 tablespoon salt

1 tablespoon olive oil

⅓ cup (60 g) minced white onion

2 teaspoons minced garlic

2 teaspoons tomato bouillon

1½ cups (350 ml) Red Chile Sauce (page 17)

6 bolillos, homemade (page 232) or store-bought, toasted, and butter, for serving

Pour the chacales into a sieve and rinse well under cold running water.

In a 4-quart (4-l) pot, combine 11 cups (2.6 l) of the water, the chacales, and salt and bring to a boil over high heat. Reduce the heat to medium and simmer uncovered, stirring occasionally and adding more water if needed to to keep the chacales covered by at least 2 inches (5 cm), for 2½ hours. The corn should be soft and tender at the end of this time.

In a small frying pan over medium heat, warm the oil. Add the onion and cook, stirring, until translucent, about 2 minutes. Add the garlic and cook, stirring, for 1 minute longer.

Add the onion and garlic to the soup pot along with the bouillon, chile sauce, and the remaining 2 cups (475 ml) water and stir well, adding more water if a thinner soup consistency is desired. Raise the heat to medium-high and bring to a boil, stirring often. Reduce the heat to low and simmer gently, stirring occasionally, for 30 minutes to blend the flavors. Taste and adjust the seasoning with salt if needed. This soup thickens as it cools.

Ladle the soup into bowls and serve at once with the bolillos and butter.

SPINACH & BEAN
Tacos

My grandma was always clever at turning one dish into many others. Take simple pinto beans as an example: she would turn *frijoles de la olla* into a completely different meal by cooking them with onion and garlic, adding spinach, and then tucking the warm mixture into charred corn tortillas. She also often cooked plant-based dishes before it was trendy. We just never called them vegetarian when I was growing up. Her saying was always, *para que rinda*, which means to add to it—to make it go further. In this case, she added canned spinach, which made this dish not only healthy but also economical to feed company. Nowadays, I use fresh spinach, but feel free to use canned or frozen.

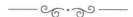

MAKES 2 SERVINGS

FRIJOLES DE LA OLLA

2 cups (400 g) dried pinto beans

¼ white onion (optional)

Salt

BEANS WITH SPINACH

1 tablespoon olive oil

½ cup (80 g) chopped white onion

2 cloves garlic, chopped

8 cups (225 g) fresh spinach, or ½ package (10 oz/285 g) frozen spinach, thawed and drained

1 cup (170 g) cooked Frijoles de la Olla, plus ⅓ cup (80 ml) cooking liquid

¼ teaspoon salt

1 tablespoon red pepper flakes (optional)

6 corn tortillas, warmed

To make the frijoles de la olla, spread the beans on a work surface so you can look for any that are broken, discolored, or shriveled. There may also be small stones or grit. Pick out and discard all the undesirable bits.

Put the beans into a colander and rinse thoroughly under cold running water. Transfer the beans to a large pot, add water to cover by 3 inches (7.5 cm), and bring to a boil over medium-high heat. Reduce the heat to medium, cover, and simmer, stirring occasionally to prevent sticking, until the beans are tender, 3–4 hours. As the beans absorb the liquid, add more hot water to cover by at least 2 inches (5 cm). Every pot is different, so begin checking the beans after 2 hours. They will usually take 3–4 hours, but I have a pot I love to use for cooking beans because the beans are always ready in only about 2 hours. About 1 hour before the beans are ready, add the onion, if using, and about 2 teaspoons salt.

When the beans are tender, remove from the heat. To store, let cool to room temperature, then transfer the beans with their liquid to as many airtight containers as you like and refrigerate for up to 5 days or freeze for up to 6 months. You should have about 5 ½ cups.

To make the beans with spinach, heat a large frying pan over medium-high heat. When the pan is hot, add the oil and swirl the pan to coat the bottom evenly. Add the onion and cook, stirring occasionally, until translucent, about 3 minutes. Add the garlic and cook, stirring, for 30 seconds. If using fresh spinach, add it to the pan in a few batches, letting each batch begin to wilt before adding

COOK'S NOTE: To cook the frijoles de la olla in an Instant Pot, combine the picked over and rinsed beans, onion (if using), salt, and 8 cups (2 l) water in the pot. Lock the lid in place, select the manual setting, and cook on high pressure for 30 minutes, then allow the pressure to release naturally, 30–40 minutes.

more, and cook, stirring occasionally, until wilted, 2–3 minutes. If using frozen spinach, add it to the pan and cook, stirring, until heated through. Stir in the beans and the cooking liquid and salt and cook, stirring often, until the most of the liquid evaporates and the beans are thoroughly heated, about 5 minutes. Sprinkle with the pepper flakes, if using, and stir to mix.

Top the warmed tortillas with the hot bean and spinach mixture, dividing it evenly, then fold in half and serve.

Al pan pan,
y al vino vino

VERACRUZ-STYLE

Tilapia

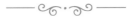

If I need to make an easy fish dish during the Lenten season, this is it. It is beyond flavorful and takes little more than a half hour to assemble and bake. More than likely I have all the ingredients on hand, and it's just a matter of purchasing fresh fish.

MAKES 4 SERVINGS

3 tablespoons olive oil

1⅔ cups (285 g) cherry tomatoes, halved

4 cloves garlic, thinly sliced

½ cup (70 g) pitted green olives, sliced

¼ cup (40 g) capers

½ cup (50 g) sliced pickled jalapeños, homemade (page 161) or store-bought (optional)

½ cup (120 ml) dry white wine

4 tilapia fillets, ¼ lb (115 g) each

1 teaspoon chile-lime seasoning, such as Tajín Clásico, plus more for serving

1 teaspoon dried Mexican oregano

Sea salt

Fresh cilantro leaves, for garnish (optional)

Lemon wedges, for serving

Preheat the oven to 350°F (180°C).

In a large frying pan over medium heat, warm 2 tablespoons of the oil. Add the tomatoes and cook, stirring occasionally, until softened and the skins begin to split, 4–5 minutes. Add the garlic and cook, stirring, until fragrant, about 1 minute. Remove from the heat and transfer to a shallow baking dish or pan just large enough to hold the fish pieces in a single layer. Add the olives, capers, jalapeños (if using), and wine to the tomato mixture and stir to mix.

Drizzle the remaining 1 tablespoon oil over the fish pieces, coating both sides, then season both sides with the chile-lime seasoning, oregano, and about ¼ teaspoon salt. Arrange the fish pieces on top of the tomato mixture and then spoon some of the tomato mixture on top of the fish.

Bake the fish until it flakes easily when tested with a fork, 15–20 minutes. The cooking time will depend on the thickness of the fish. Remove from the oven and sprinkle with more chile-lime seasoning and/or salt and the cilantro, if using. Serve with the lemon wedges.

COOK'S NOTE: You can also use this baked fish as a taco filling. Top warmed corn tortillas with the fish and its vegetables, garnish with your favorite toppings, and serve with your salsa of choice and lemon wedges.

MAR Y TIERRA
Molcajete

Surf and turf—don't let the name fool you. This hot stone bowl is meat-free.
Instead of grilled steak, this *molcajete* has portobello mushrooms. A *molcajete* is the traditional
Mexican lava-rock mortar used for grinding dried chiles and spices and for making salsas
and guacamole. It also makes an excellent serving vessel, as the rock conducts and holds heat
well, keeping the dish piping hot at the table, and dishes served in it are called *molcajetes*.
This bubbling *molcajete* combines shrimp and mushrooms with bell peppers, spring onions,
and nopales in a spicy salsa of your choice and is served with panela cheese and tortillas.

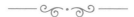

MAKES 2 SERVINGS

¼ cup (60 ml) extra-virgin
olive oil

1 tablespoon balsamic vinegar

1 tablespoon reduced-sodium
soy sauce or Maggi Seasoning

2 nopales (cactus paddles)

1 red bell pepper, halved
and seeded

2 large portobello mushrooms,
brushed clean

2 spring onions or large green
onions, root ends trimmed

1 jalapeño chile (optional)

¼ lb (115 g) large shrimp,
peeled and deveined with tail
segment intact

Salt and ground black pepper

1 cup Salsa de Molcajete (page
165), Roasted Tomatillo Salsa
(page 17), or Red Chile Sauce
(page 17), warmed

¼ lb (115 g) queso panela,
thickly sliced, or queso fresco,
crumbled

Flour or corn tortillas,
warmed, for serving

Preheat the oven to 200°F (95°C). Set a large molcajete on a sheet
pan and place in the oven to heat.

In a small bowl, whisk together the oil, vinegar, and soy sauce and
set aside.

To prepare each nopal, grasp the base and, using a sharp paring
knife, scrape off all the spines, moving the blade away from the base.
Repeat on the other side, then trim off the base and all the edges.

Line a large sheet pan with aluminum foil or parchment paper
and arrange the nopales, bell pepper, mushrooms, onions, jalapeño
(if using), and shrimp in a single layer on the pan. Brush all the
vegetables and the shrimp liberally with the oil mixture, coating
both sides, and then generously sprinkle on both sides with salt
and pepper.

Prepare a charcoal or gas grill for direct grilling over medium-high
heat, or preheat a stove-top grill pan over medium-high heat. Working
in batches as needed to avoid crowding, grill all the vegetables, turning
once, until just tender and lightly charred, 2–3 minutes on each side.
Grill the shrimp, turning once, until opaque and lightly charred,
1–2 minutes on each side. Cut the mushrooms and bell pepper into
slices 1 inch (2.5 cm) wide and halve the jalapeño lengthwise, if using.

Wearing oven mitts, carefully remove the hot molcajete from the
oven. Lay the nopales and bell pepper slices in the molcajete so they
extend over the rim. Arrange the cheese, shrimp, mushrooms, and
onions in the molcajete, then ladle the warm salsa over the top. Serve
at once with the jalapeño, if using, and tortillas.

TRES LECHES BREAD PUDDING
with Bourbon Sauce

Mexican bread pudding, or *capirotada*, is a very special dish that I look forward to every Lenten season. My grandma and mom always made *capirotada* with cinnamon, *piloncillo*, cloves, raisins, cheese, and bread. In my recipe, I skip the cheese, and I soak the bread in a *tres leches* mixture in addition to the traditional cinnamon-infused *piloncillo* syrup, plus I soak the raisins in bourbon. But the richness doesn't end there. When the pudding emerges from the oven, I drizzle a bourbon sauce on top. Even though my mom is a traditionalist, she admitted that she is impressed and *might* even prefer my modern boozy *capirotada*, but that could have been the bourbon talking.

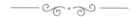

MAKE 8–10 SERVINGS

3½ cups (825 ml) water

½ lb (225 g) piloncillo, coarsely chopped, or 1 cup (210 g) packed dark brown sugar

4 cinnamon sticks

5 whole cloves

1 cup (160 g) raisins

1 cup (240 ml) bourbon

5 bolillos, homemade (page 232) or store-bought, or 1½ large baguettes

½ cup (115 g) unsalted butter, melted

⅔ cup (160 ml) whole milk

2 cups (475 ml) sweetened condensed milk

1 cup (240 ml) evaporated milk

In a large saucepan, combine the water, piloncillo, cinnamon, and cloves and bring to a boil over medium-high heat, stirring to dissolve piloncillo. Reduce the heat to low and simmer, stirring often, until a slightly thick syrup forms, about 5 minutes. Remove from the heat, cover, and set aside to steep for 30 minutes. Pour through a fine-mesh sieve and discard the cinnamon and cloves. Set aside until needed.

While the syrup is steeping, in a bowl, combine the raisins and bourbon and let soak for 1 hour.

Position 2 oven racks in the center of the oven and preheat the oven to 350°F (180°C).

Cut the bolillos into slices ½ inch (12 mm) thick. Brush the slices on both sides with the butter, arranging them in single layer on 2 sheet pans as they are ready. Bake the slices for 8 minutes, then switch the pans between the oven racks and continue to bake until lightly golden, about 5 minutes longer. Set aside. Leave the oven on.

While the bread is toasting, in a bowl, combine the whole, condensed, and evaporated milks. Drain the raisins into a sieve held over the bowl and set the raisins aside. Stir together the milks and bourbon.

Spray the bottom and sides of an 8½ x 12½-inch (21.5 x 31.5-cm) baking dish with cooking spray. Layer the ingredients in the prepared dish in the following order: one-third of the toasted bread, one-third of the raisins, 1⅓ cups (325 ml) of the syrup, and 1⅓ cups (325 ml) of the milk mixture, pouring the liquids evenly over the toasted

Nonstick cooking spray, for the baking dish and foil

½ cup (60 g) pecans, chopped (optional)

BOURBON SAUCE

4 tablespoons (60 g) unsalted butter

Pinch of salt

1 cup (240 ml) sweetened condensed milk

3 tablespoons bourbon

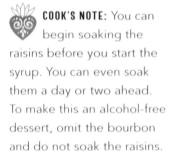 **COOK'S NOTE:** You can begin soaking the raisins before you start the syrup. You can even soak them a day or two ahead. To make this an alcohol-free dessert, omit the bourbon and do not soak the raisins.

bread. Wait for 15 minutes. Now, layer another one-third of the bread, one-third of the raisins, 1⅓ cups (325 ml) of the syrup, and 1⅓ cups (325 ml) of the milk mixture. Let soak again for 15 minutes. Top with the remaining bread, raisins, syrup, and milk mixture and let soak for a final 15 minutes.

Sprinkle the top layer with the pecans, if using. Cover the dish with aluminum foil that has been sprayed with cooking spray and bake for 40 minutes. Uncover the dish and continue to bake until the top is golden brown, 10–15 minutes more.

While the capirotada is baking, make the bourbon sauce. In a saucepan over low heat, melt the butter with the salt and stir to mix. Remove from the heat, add the condensed milk and bourbon, and stir until fully incorporated and smooth.

When the pudding is ready, remove from the oven and let cool slightly before serving. The capirotada can be served warm or at room temperature. Serve the bourbon sauce in a small pitcher on the side for pouring on to taste.

Clothespin Cross

Anyone who knows me knows that I appreciate sacred art. So when my mom showed me how cute and simple these wooden crosses are to make, I knew I wanted to share this craft for the Lenten season. Have you ever seen anything like this? Most people do a double take once they realize these crosses are made out of clothespins. The possibilities for decorating and displaying these unique crosses are many. Some crafters get very fancy with extras like sequins, beads, and colorful ribbons and string. Small crosses outfitted with a ribbon loop make attractive hanging ornaments. Have fun!

Materials

Large piece of cardboard or a cutting board

Aluminum foil

16 or more wooden clothespins with metal springs, natural or stained

Hot glue

Small saw or serrated knife, for trimming

Mod Podge and foam paintbrush (optional)

Wrap the cardboard with aluminum foil for a mess-free work surface. Carefully take each clothespin apart, removing the metal spring. Then, using the glue gun, reassemble each pin and glue the two pieces together. If needed, use the small saw to carefully trim the clothespins.

Once you have glued together each clothespin, arrange the pins in a cross design of your choice and glue them together. Here are two of my favorite designs.

If you like, using the Mod Podge and a foam paintbrush, seal the front of the cross to preserve the wood color and to give it a slightly shiny finish. Let the cross dry for at least 1 hour on each side in a well-ventilated area.

VALENTINE'S
Day

As my grandma Jesusita used to say. *Panza llena, corazón contento,* which means "full stomach, happy heart." I couldn't agree more! During the season of *amor,* try making any of these delicious treats to show your loved ones how truly special they are.

When my kids were little, I usually made a family dinner on Valentine's Day—steak and lobster or crab legs—for all of us to enjoy. Sometimes we shared our dinner table with another family or couple. While I've always heard that food is the way to a man's heart, sharing the table is my favorite way to show everyone my love. As the great labor leader Cesar Chavez once said, "The people who give you their food give you their heart."

Now that the kids are older, my hubby and I like to enjoy a romantic dinner out, usually dining on sushi. However you choose to celebrate this holiday, make sure there is something sweet and special for the occasion. Preparing holiday treats from scratch doesn't have to be difficult or expensive. Make a batch of my Heart-Shaped Berry Empanadas or Cajeta Thumbprint Cookies for your children's lunch box or for their Valentine's Day classroom party. If you are celebrating Valentine's Day with *amigas,* mix up some chocolate martinis and a batch of Dulce de Leche Brownies to spread the love. To celebrate the day with your partner, there is no better ending to a delicious meal than my luscious Chocolate Mousse. And don't forget to toast your love with my gorgeous Passion Fruit Margarita!

No matter how you celebrate this day of adoration, these simple and sweet recipes are the ideal way to say "I love you."

Panza llena,
corazón contento

CHEESE BOARD

If you ever come to my home, I can guarantee you there will be a fruit and cheese platter to nibble on. It's my go-to spread that doesn't take much effort but looks impressive. For Christmas, I like to arrange the fruit and cheese in the shape of a holiday tree or wreath, and in the summer, I often grill the fruit slices. For the Fourth of July, I decorate with festive red, white, and blue fruits, and for Halloween, I like to add plastic spiders and cute ghost-shaped fried tortillas. For Valentine's Day, I keep it simple and decorate with edible flowers and butterfly- or heart-shaped butter crackers.

I am dedicating this Valentine's Day cheese board to my daughter, Maya, and her love of cheese. From the time she was a little girl, she loved to sample cheeses and could taste the difference between a Gruyère and an Emmentaler blindfolded. Together we selected some of our favorite fruits and cheeses for this simple cheese board. Plan on about 2 ounces (60 g) cheese per person. Anytime we go to a Latin market, we buy a block each of quince paste and guava paste. Both taste great sliced and served alongside cheese.

—— ⌖ ——

Peach slices, pear slices, or strawberries

Apple slices

Ate de membrillo (quince paste)

Ate de guayaba (guava paste)

Assorted soft and hard cheeses

    Requesón (ricotta)
    Asadero or Oaxaca
    Manchego
    Cabernet

Water crackers or crackers of choice

Honeycomb

Edible flowers and fresh herbs

Arrange the fruit slices, fruit pastes, cheeses, crackers, and honeycomb on a large wooden board. Tuck in the flowers and herbs for color.

"The people who give you their food give you their heart."
~Cesar Chavez

HEART-SHAPED BERRY
Empanadas

If you ask my son, Blake, what he wants his *abuela* to make for him, he always says empanadas. Empanadas were very special for me growing up too. I loved helping my grandma make them, and now my son loves to help make them with his grandma. But more importantly, he loves to eat them and share them with friends at school. These heart-shaped empanadas are bursting with a deep purple filling of freshly cooked blueberries and strawberries and are finished with a drizzle of pastel pink strawberry glaze.

MAKES ABOUT 18 EMPANADAS

BERRY FILLING

1 teaspoon water

⅛ teaspoon salt

½ cup (100 g) granulated sugar

¾ lb (340 g) blueberries (2⅓ cups)

¾ lb (340 g) strawberries (2⅓ cups), stemmed and cored

½ teaspoon vanilla paste or pure vanilla extract

3 tablespoons cornstarch

EMPANADA DOUGH

3 cups (375 g) all-purpose flour, plus more for dusting

2 teaspoons baking powder

½ teaspoon salt

2 tablespoons granulated sugar

1 teaspoon ground cinnamon

½ cup (115 g) solid vegetable shortening, at room temperature

2 large eggs

½ cup (120 ml) buttermilk

Continues on the following page

To make the filling, in a heavy-bottomed saucepan over medium heat, combine the water, salt, and granulated sugar and heat, stirring, until the sugar dissolves, about 2 minutes. Reduce the heat to medium-low, add the blueberries, strawberries, and vanilla, and cook, stirring occasionally, until the berries are soft, about 5 minutes.

Remove from the heat. Using a potato masher, mash the berries. Spoon out the liquid into a small bowl and set aside to cool, then stir the cornstarch into the liquid to make a slurry.

Add the slurry to the mashed berries, return the pan to low heat, and cook, stirring, until the filling thickens, about 3 minutes. Remove from the heat, cover, and refrigerate until cold before using.

To make the dough, in a large bowl, stir together the flour, baking powder, salt, granulated sugar, and cinnamon. Add the shortening and, using a pastry blender, work the shortening into the flour mixture until a crumbly consistency forms. In a small bowl, whisk together the eggs and buttermilk. Pour the egg mixture into the flour mixture and stir and toss with a fork until a rough dough comes together. (The dough can also be made in a stand mixer fitted with the paddle attachment, using low speed for both steps.)

Divide the dough in half, wrap each half in plastic wrap, and refrigerate both halves for 20–30 minutes.

Continued from the previous page

Whole or evaporated milk, for brushing

1 large egg beaten with 2 tablespoons water, for the egg wash

Turbinado sugar, for sprinkling

Nonstick cooking spray, for the sheet pan

STRAWBERRY GLAZE (OPTIONAL)

4 strawberries, stemmed, cored, and chopped

1 tablespoon fresh lemon juice

1 tablespoon water

1½ cup–2 cups (170–225 g) confectioners' sugar

 COOK'S NOTES: No buttermilk on hand? Add 1½ teaspoons distilled white vinegar or fresh lemon juice to ½ cup (120 ml) milk. Stir gently and then let sit for about 5 minutes before using.

Leftover empanadas will keep in an airtight container in the refrigerator for a few days. Reheat them in a preheated 350°F (180°C) oven for 8 minutes.

To assemble and bake the empanadas, position 1 oven rack in the center of the oven and 1 rack in the top third of the oven and preheat the oven to 350°F (180°C). Remove half of the dough from the refrigerator, divide it into 12 equal pieces, and shape each piece into a ball. Keep the balls covered with a kitchen towel when you are not working with them.

On a lightly floured work surface, one at a time, roll out each dough ball into a round ⅛ inch (3 mm) thick. Using a 3½–4-inch (8.5–10-cm) heart-shaped cookie cutter, cut out a heart shape from each dough round. Gather up the dough scraps and set aside. Lightly brush half of the hearts with milk and top each one with about 2 tablespoons of the filling. Cover with a second heart and seal the edges securely by pressing with the tines of a fork. Repeat with the remaining dough half and filling, then press together the scraps, roll out, and cut out and fill more hearts.

Brush each empanada with a little of the egg wash and then lightly sprinkle with a little turbinado sugar. Puncture the top of each empanada twice with the tines of a fork to allow steam to escape during baking.

Spray a large sheet pan with cooking spray. Carefully transfer the empanadas to the prepared sheet pan, spacing them about 1 inch (2.5 cm) apart. Place the pan on the center oven rack and bake the empanadas for 12 minutes. Move the pan to the top rack and continue to bake until golden brown, 3–5 minutes.

While the empanadas are baking, make the glaze. In a small saucepan over medium heat, combine the berries, lemon juice, and water and heat until the berries begin to release their juices, about 5 minutes. Remove from the heat and, using the potato masher, mash the berries, then transfer to a bowl and let cool. Whisk the confectioners' sugar into the cooled berries, about ½ cup (60 g) at a time, until smooth, using only as much sugar as you need to achieve a good drizzling consistency.

When the empanadas are ready, remove from the oven and let cool on a wire rack for about 15 minutes, then drizzle with the glaze and let cool until set, about 1 hour. Enjoy the empanadas warm or at room temperature.

CAJETA
Thumbprint Cookies

These buttery cookies are favorites of children and grown-ups alike—the perfect Valentine's Day dessert for a school lunch box or a romantic dessert. *Cajeta* is similar to *dulce de leche*, a popular Latin American caramel-like sauce, but instead of being made with cow's milk, it is made with goat's milk. I finish these cookies with a sprinkle of coarse salt, which nicely balances the sweetness of the *cajeta*.

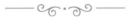

MAKES 12 COOKIES

1 cup (125 g) all-purpose flour

2 tablespoons cornstarch

⅛ teaspoon kosher salt

½ cup (115 g) unsalted butter, at room temperature

½ cup (60 g) confectioners' sugar

1 large egg yolk

1 tablespoon pure vanilla extract

About 2 tablespoons cajeta, preferably in a squeeze bottle, for topping

Coarse salt, for sprinkling (optional)

Preheat the oven to 350°F (180°C). Line a sheet pan with parchment paper.

In a small bowl, stir together the flour, cornstarch, and salt. In a medium bowl, using an electric mixer, beat together the butter and sugar on medium speed until light and fluffy. Add the egg yolk and vanilla and beat until well combined. On low speed, add the flour mixture and beat just until incorporated.

To form each cookie, scoop up a spoonful of the dough, roll it between your palms into a smooth ball, and place on the prepared sheet pan, spacing the balls about 2 inches (5 cm) apart. You should have 12 balls. Using your thumb or the end of a wooden spoon, create a heart shape about ¼ inch (6 mm) deep in the center of each ball.

Bake the cookies until the bottoms are light golden brown, 14–15 minutes. Let cool on the pan on a wire rack for 10 minutes, then fill each heart with ½ teaspoon of the cajeta and top with a tiny pinch of the salt, if using. Let cool completely before serving. The cookies will keep in an airtight container at room temperature for up to 3 days.

 COOK'S NOTE: Dulce de leche can be substituted for the cajeta. The recipe doubles easily for a party.

DULCE DE LECHE
Brownies

Dulce de leche is basically sugar and milk (or, for a shortcut, sweetened condensed milk) that is slowly cooked until it caramelizes. Although you can make *dulce de leche* at home, these brownies work great with a store-bought product. You will likely have all the ingredients on hand for this recipe when the craving for a sweet hits, and fortunately the batter goes together quickly and easily. The hardest part is having to wait until the brownies chill for an hour before you can eat them.

MAKES 9 LARGE OR 16 SMALL BROWNIES

Nonstick cooking spray, for the pan

½ cup (60 g) all-purpose flour

1 tablespoon cornstarch

½ teaspoon ground cinnamon

¼ teaspoon salt

⅛ teaspoon baking soda

1¼ cups (250 g) granulated sugar

5 tablespoons (75 g) unsalted butter

2 large eggs plus 1 large egg yolk, cold

1 teaspoon pure vanilla extract

⅓ cup (80 ml) vegetable oil

¾ cup (70 g) unsweetened cocoa powder

¾ cup (130 g) semisweet chocolate chips

⅔ cup (200 g) dulce de leche

Preheat the oven to 325°F (165°C). Line the bottom and sides of an 8-inch (20-cm) square pan with parchment paper, allowing it to extend beyond the rim by about 1 inch (2.5 cm), then spray with cooking spray.

In a small bowl, whisk together the flour, constarch, cinnamon, salt, and baking soda. In a medium microwave-safe bowl, combine the sugar and butter and microwave on medium power just until the butter is melted, about 1 minute. Whisk in the eggs, egg yolk, and vanilla. Stir in the oil and cocoa powder until the cocoa dissolves and the mixture is smooth. Add the flour mixture and stir until fully incorporated. Stir in the chocolate chips, distributing them evenly.

Spread half of the batter evenly in the bottom of the prepared pan and bake for 10 minutes. Remove from the oven. Dollop the dulce de leche on top of the baked brownie batter, portioning it in 9 evenly spaced spoonfuls, and then top evenly with the remaining batter. Using a knife, swirl together the top brownie layer and the dulce de leche layer.

Return the pan to the oven and bake for about 20 minutes longer. The top should feel just barely set to the touch. Do not overbake. Let cool completely in the pan on a wire rack, then cover and refrigerate for at least 1 hour before serving.

Using the edges of the parchment, lift the brownies out of the pan, then cut into squares to serve. The brownies will keep in an airtight container at room temperature for up to 3 days.

CHOCOLATE
Mousse

If you love Mexican chocolate, you will love this light, creamy mousse, which has hints of chipotle, cinnamon, and vanilla. This mousse tastes beyond fancy but is quite easy to make.

— ❦ • ❧ —

MAKES 4–6 SERVINGS

1 cup (240 ml) heavy cream, cold

4½ oz (130 g) bittersweet chocolate, preferably 70 percent cacao, finely chopped

2 tablespoons unsalted butter, cubed

2 tablespoons brewed espresso or very strong coffee

3 large eggs, separated

1 tablespoon superfine sugar

1 teaspoon pure vanilla extract

¾ teaspoon ground chipotle chile

1 teaspoon ground cinnamon

CHANTILLY CREAM

1 cup (240 ml) heavy cream, cold

1½ teaspoons pure vanilla extract

1 tablespoon superfine sugar

Shaved or grated Mexican chocolate, for serving

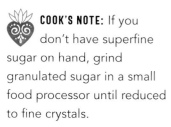 **COOK'S NOTE:** If you don't have superfine sugar on hand, grind granulated sugar in a small food processor until reduced to fine crystals.

In a bowl, using an electric mixer, beat the cream on medium-high speed until soft peaks form. Cover and refrigerate until needed.

In the top pan of a double boiler, combine the chocolate, butter, and espresso. Place over (not touching) hot, steamy (not simmering) water in the lower pan and heat, stirring frequently, until smooth. Remove the chocolate mixture from the heat and let cool until just warm to the touch. Do not allow the chocolate mixture to get too cool or lumps will form when the other ingredients are added.

Meanwhile, in a bowl, using the electric mixer with clean beaters, beat the egg whites on medium speed until they are foamy and beginning to hold a shape. Sprinkle in the sugar, increase the speed to medium-high, and continue to beat until the whites form stiff, glossy peaks.

When the chocolate mixture is just warm to the touch, in a small bowl, whisk the egg yolks until blended, then stir them into the chocolate mixture, mixing well. Gently stir in about one-third of the whipped cream to thin and loosen the chocolate mixture. Fold in half of the egg whites just until incorporated, then gently fold in the remaining egg whites just until mixed. Finally, fold in the remaining whipped cream just until no white streaks remain.

Spoon the mousse into individual serving dishes, cover, and refrigerate for at least 8 hours or for up to 24 hours.

Just before you are ready to serve the mousse, make the Chantilly cream. In a bowl, using the electric mixer, beat together the cream, vanilla, and superfine sugar on medium-high speed until soft peaks form.

Top each serving of mousse with the Chantilly cream and a dusting of chocolate shavings.

MEXICAN CHOCOLATE
Martini

My hubby loves sweet drinks, while I'm more of a margarita kinda gal. He's a huge fan of chocolate martinis, so I knew I had to make one for him, but with a Latin twist, of course. This is a great martini not only for Valentine's Day but for any special occasion.

MAKES 2 COCKTAILS

4 fl oz (120 ml) Baileys Irish Cream

4 fl oz (120 ml) crème de cacao

4 fl oz (120 ml) vodka

Ice cubes

Grated Mexican chocolate, for garnish

In a cocktail shaker, combine the Baileys Irish Cream, crème de cacao, and vodka, then fill two-thirds full with ice. Cover and shake vigorously until the outside of the shaker is lightly frosted. Strain the mixture into 2 martini glasses, dividing it evenly.

Garnish with the chocolate and serve.

PASSION FRUIT
Margarita

I use fresh passion fruit for this cocktail, but if you can't find fresh fruits, you can substitute with store-bought passion fruit pulp (purée). Drink this margarita with caution, as it is silky smooth and goes down very easily.

MAKES 2 COCKTAILS

2 passion fruits, or 3 fl oz (45 ml) passion fruit pulp (purée)

Juice of 2 limes

8 fl oz (240 ml) passion fruit juice or pineapple juice

4 fl oz (120 ml) tequila blanco

Ice cubes

Halve the passion fruits and scoop the flesh into 2 short tumblers, dividing it evenly, or evenly divide the purchased fruit pulp between the glasses. Divide the lime juice, passion fruit juice, and tequila evenly between the glasses and stir to mix. Top off with ice and serve.

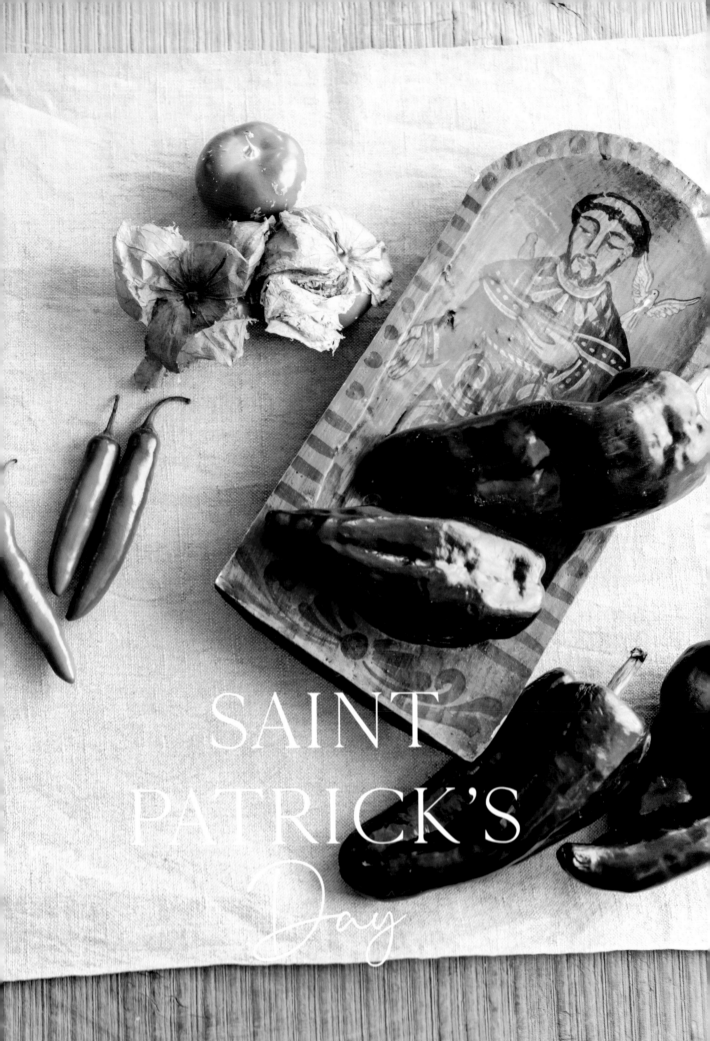

SAINT
PATRICK'S
Day

Growing up Mexican American, my family did not celebrate Saint Patrick's Day. The only thing I remember was kids pinching me at school when I didn't wear green. I didn't really know anything else about the holiday.

That all changed once my hubby (who is a wee bit Irish) introduced me to popular Irish dishes. Now we eat corned beef brisket ever year, and in this cookbook, I have turned that traditional Irish dish into tacos with lots of festive green toppings. Here you'll also find a Mexican chocolate stout cake glazed with whiskey-infused ganache that honors both cultures. This new family tradition—celebrating Saint Patrick's Day with a Mexican twist—is one that my beautifully blended mixed-heritage children anticipate with joy.

When I learned that Mexican and Irish people have two important things in common, it changed my perspective on celebrating what once felt like a foreign holiday. The first is our shared religious tradition of Catholicism, which dates to the early sixteenth century in Mexico and the early fifth century in Ireland. The second is emigration from their homeland, with many immigrants from both countries settling down in the United States.

If you, too, wish to celebrate Saint Patrick's Day—because everybody is a wee bit Irish on Saint Patrick's Day—here is a collection of my favorite Irish-Mexican fusion recipes to see you through. If you're feeling spunky, start and end your day with a steaming cup of *café de olla* spiked with creamy Irish liqueur and be sure to toast to your health in both Irish and Spanish, *Sláinte! Salud!* Next, dress your plate in green with Pipián Verde, or go for gold with my cozy Mexican Beef and Guinness Stew. Either way, sop up the last bits of goodness with my green chile–laced Irish soda bread.

No matter what you choose to make, these delicious recipes are sure to "sham-rock your world!" Here's to wishing you and yours a pot of gold and all the love your hearts can hold.

MEXICAN BEEF
& Guinness Stew

On Sundays, my grandma often had a stew slow cooking in an electric roaster sitting atop the yellow clothes dryer in her kitchen. If I close my eyes, I can smell my grandma's *cocina* filled with delicious aromas and hear a house full of laughter. How that small roasting pan filled with stew served so many visitors I'll never know. This stew is inspired by my grandma's recipe, but I flavor it with Guinness stout to give it an Irish accent.

MAKES 8 SERVINGS

5 tablespoons (75 ml) olive oil

2 lb (1 kg) boneless beef chuck roast or chuck steak, cut into 1-inch (2.5-cm) cubes

¾ teaspoon salt

2 teaspoons ground black pepper

1 yellow onion, chopped

4 cloves garlic, minced

¼ cup (30 g) all-purpose flour

2 cups (475 ml) water

½–1 cup (120–240 ml) Guinness stout

3 cups (700 ml) low-sodium beef broth, plus more if needed

1 bay leaf

2 russet potatoes, peeled and cut into 1-inch (2.5-cm) chunks

3 carrots, peeled and cut into 1-inch (2.5-cm) chunks

Irish soda bread, homemade (page 62) or store-bought, for serving

In a large frying pan over medium-high heat, warm 1 tablespoon of the oil. While the oil is heating, season the beef with the salt and pepper. Working in two batches to avoid crowding, add the beef to the pan and cook, turning once, until browned on both sides, 2–3 minutes on each side. Transfer the beef to a plate. Repeat with the remaining beef, adding 1 tablespoon of the oil to the pan. Set the beef aside.

Return the pan to medium heat and add the remaining 3 tablespoons oil to the drippings in the pan. When the oil is hot, add the onion and cook, stirring often, until translucent, 2–3 minutes. Add the garlic and cook, stirring, for 1 minute. Remove the pan from the heat.

Place a large pot over medium-high heat and add the browned meat. Sprinkle with the flour and cook, stirring often, for 3 minutes. Add the water, ½ cup (120 ml) of the stout, the broth, bay leaf, and the onion and drippings from the frying pan, stir well, and bring to a boil. Reduce the heat to medium and simmer uncovered for 30 minutes.

If the cooking liquid is too thick, add the remaining ½ cup (120 ml) stout or more broth. Then add the potatoes and carrots and continue to simmer until the vegetables and meat are tender, 15–20 minutes. Taste and adjust the seasoning with salt and pepper if needed.

Serve the stew piping hot with the bread on the side.

 COOK'S NOTE: The alcohol in the stout cooks off, which makes this stew safe to serve to kids.

CORNED BEEF *Brisket Tacos*

This boldly seasoned corned beef brisket can be sliced and served as a traditional Saint Patrick's Day main course. But it is even tastier shredded and tucked into tortillas (especially my homemade green ones!) for a fusion of Ireland and Mexico in one amazing taco! I have used a slow cooker here, but it can also be roasted in the oven (see Cook's Note). For the beer, choose a stout, ale, or lager.

—— ✽ ——

MAKES 4–6 SERVINGS

BRISKET

1 corned beef brisket, 2–3 lb (1–1.4 kg), with spice packet

¼ cup (40 g) granulated piloncillo or (60 g) packed dark brown sugar

2 teaspoons ground ancho chile

1½ teaspoons salt

1 teaspoon black peppercorns

2 bay leaves

3 fresh thyme sprigs

1 large yellow onion, quartered

4 cloves garlic, peeled

2 bottles (12 fl oz/350 ml each) beer

CABBAGE SLAW

2 cups (170 g) shredded green cabbage

½ cup (15 g) fresh flat-leaf parsley leaves, chopped

2 green onions, sliced

¼ cup (60 ml) mayonnaise

1 tablespoon sour cream

1 teaspoon cider vinegar

1 teaspoon granulated sugar

Salt and ground black pepper

12 corn tortillas, homemade (page 206) or store-bought, warmed

Fresh flat-leaf parsley sprigs, jalapeño slices, and lime quarters, for serving

To prepare the brisket, rinse it under cool running water to remove the excess salt. Put it, fat side up, into a slow cooker and sprinkle with the contents of the spice packet. Then sprinkle the piloncillo, ancho chile, salt, and peppercorns over the meat and top with the bay leaves and thyme sprigs, followed by the onion quarters and garlic. Pour in the beer. If needed, add water to cover the brisket by 1 inch (2.5 cm). Cover and cook on the low setting until fork-tender, 8–10 hours.

Transfer the corned beef to a cutting board and let rest for a few minutes to firm up, then shred the meat and keep warm.

While the brisket is resting, make the slaw. In a small bowl, toss together the cabbage, parsley, and green onions. In a second small bowl, stir together the mayonnaise, sour cream, vinegar, and sugar, mixing well. Pour the mayonnaise mixture over the cabbage mixture and toss to mix well. Season with salt and pepper.

Arrange the corned beef on the warm tortillas, top with the cabbage slaw, and then with all the green garnishes: parsley, and jalapeño slices. Fold and serve with the limes on the side for everyone to add lime juice to taste.

COOK'S NOTE: To cook the corned beef brisket in the oven, preheat the oven to 350°F (180°C). In a Dutch oven or deep baking dish, combine all the ingredients as directed. Cover with a lid or aluminum foil and bake until fork-tender, about 1 hour per pound (450 g).

PIPIÁN VERDE

A pipián is a sauce made with seeds (and sometimes nuts) and vegetables. Pipianes come in red (rojo) and green (verde) versions, and although similar to moles, they tend to be simpler to make. Bright, thick, rich, and spicy, this green pipián, which is sometimes called green mole, is packed with tangy tomatillos, roasted poblanos, jalapeños, and toasted pumpkin seeds. It is delicious spooned over roasted turkey (page 240) or carnitas (page 145), can be used for enchiladas (page 18) or chilaquiles (page 16), or can be spooned over roasted chicken and served with rice and corn tortillas.

─── ⚬₰•₰⚬ ───

MAKES ABOUT 4 CUPS (950 ML)

5 tomatillos, husked and rinsed

1 cup (130 g) raw pepitas
(hull-free pumpkin seeds)

3 large cloves garlic, unpeeled

½ large white onion, quartered

3 poblano chiles, roasted,
peeled, and seeded (page 15)

2 small jalapeño chiles,
stemmed and roughly chopped

1½ cups (350 ml) vegetable
or chicken broth, plus more
if needed

Leaves from ½ bunch
fresh cilantro

½ teaspoon kosher salt

Ground black pepper

2 tablespoons olive oil

COOK'S NOTE: The pepitas can be roasted in the oven instead of on the stove top. Preheat the oven to 350°F (180°C). Line a sheet pan with parchment paper and spread the pepitas on the prepared pan. Roast, stirring once after about 6 minutes, until lightly toasted, about 12 minutes. Pour onto a plate to cool.

In a saucepan over medium-high heat, combine the tomatillos with water to cover and bring to a simmer. Adjust the heat to maintain a steady simmer and cook until tender, about 15 minutes. Drain well and let cool to room temperature.

While the tomatillos are cooking, place a cast-iron frying pan over medium-high heat. When the pan is hot, pour in only enough pepitas to cover the bottom of the pan in a single layer and heat, stirring every so often with a wooden spoon. As the pepitas heat, they will puff and pop. Toast them until they turn golden brown, 3–4 minutes, then pour onto a plate and let cool completely. Repeat with the remaining pepitas. Do not leave them in the hot pan, as they will continue to toast and may burn.

Return the frying pan to medium-high heat, add the garlic and onion, and roast, turning as needed to color evenly, until lightly charred, about 8 minutes. Transfer to a plate and let cool to room temperature. Peel the garlic and discard the skins.

In a blender, combine the tomatillos, garlic, onion, poblanos, jalapeños, ¾ cup (100 g) of the pepitas, the broth, cilantro, and salt and blend until smooth. Sprinkle with pepper, blend briefly, and then taste and adjust with salt and pepper if needed.

In a heavy pot over medium-high heat, warm the oil. Carefully pour the sauce into the hot oil (it will splatter) and bring to a boil, stirring occasionally to prevent scorching. Reduce the heat to a gentle simmer, cover partially, and cook, stirring frequently, until thickened, 20–25 minutes. If you want a thinner sauce, add more broth.

Taste once again for salt and adjust if needed, then remove from the heat. Use immediately (see suggestions in the headnote), garnishing the sauce with the remaining pepitas, or let cool and store in an airtight container in the refrigerator for up to 5 days.

IRISH SODA BREAD
with Roasted Green Chile

This rustic bread calls for only a handful of ingredients and is easy to make. Best of all, yeast is not needed. If you are pressed for time, you can use canned roasted green chile. I promise not to tell anyone. No cast-iron frying pan? Make and shape the dough as directed, then place in a Dutch oven or buttered pie dish, score the top, and bake as directed.

MAKES 8–16 SERVINGS

4 tablespoons (60 g) cold unsalted butter, cubed, plus room-temperature butter for the frying pan and melted butter for the baked loaf

4¼ cups (530 g) all-purpose flour, plus more for dusting

3 tablespoons sugar

1½ teaspoons baking soda

1½ teaspoons salt

½ cup (70 g) roasted, peeled, seeded, and chopped green chile, patted dry (page 15)

1¼ cups (300 ml) buttermilk

Salted Irish butter, for serving

COOK'S NOTE: Leftover soda bread can be tightly wrapped in aluminum foil and stored at room temperature for up to 2 days or in the refrigerator for up to 1 week.

Preheat the oven to 400°F (200°C). Butter the bottom and sides of a 10–12-inch (25–30-cm) cast-iron frying pan.

In a large bowl, whisk together the flour, sugar, baking soda, and salt. Scatter the butter cubes over the flour mixture and, using a pastry blender or your fingers, work the butter into the flour mixture until the butter is in pea-size pieces. Stir in the chile, distributing it evenly.

Pour in the buttermilk, then gently fold together the liquid and dry ingredients until the dough comes together. Turn the dough out onto a lightly floured work surface and, with lightly floured hands, work the dough into a rough ball (it will be crumbly). Knead just until the dough holds together, about 30 seconds. If the dough is too sticky, work in a little more flour. Gently shape into a ball.

Transfer the dough ball to the prepared pan. Using a very sharp knife, score a deep X into the top. Bake the bread until it is golden brown and the center where it is scored appears cooked through, about 45 minutes. If the top begins to brown too much before the bread is ready, loosely cover it with aluminum foil.

Remove from the oven and brush it with the melted butter. Let cool in the pan for a few minutes, then transfer to a wire rack and let cool for at least 30 minutes before serving. Slice and serve with the Irish butter.

MEXICAN CHOCOLATE STOUT CAKE
with Irish Whiskey Ganache

This cake, with its hints of vanilla and cinnamon, is everything I love about Mexican chocolate. It is rich and flavorful, has a moist texture, and is guaranteed to impress. The whiskey ganache provides a glossy, not overly sweet finish that takes this cake over the top.

— ᜒ • ᜒ —

MAKES 12 SERVINGS

CAKE

1½ oz (45 g) Mexican chocolate

1 cup (240 ml) vegetable oil

½ cup (40 g) unsweetened cocoa powder

½ cup (120 ml) Guinness stout

Nonstick baking spray that contains flour, for the pan

2¼ cups (280 g) all-purpose flour

1 teaspoon baking soda

1 teaspoon salt

1 teaspoon ground cinnamon

2 cups (425 g) packed light brown sugar

1 tablespoon pure vanilla extract

4 large eggs, at room temperature

1 cup (225 g) sour cream, at room temperature

To make the cake, put the Mexican chocolate into a microwave-safe bowl and microwave on medium power until softened, 30–40 seconds. Transfer the chocolate to a heavy, small saucepan, add the oil and cocoa powder, and heat over medium heat, stirring occasionally, just until all the ingredients are evenly blended. Remove from the heat, add the Guinness, stir to mix, and set aside to cool slightly, 5–10 minutes.

Position an oven rack in the lower third of the oven and preheat the oven to 350°F (180°C).

Generously spray a 10–12-cup (2.4–2.8-l) Bundt pan with baking spray that contains flour.

In a bowl, whisk together the flour, baking soda, salt, and cinnamon and set aside. In a large bowl, using an electric mixer, beat together half of the chocolate mixture and the sugar on low speed until well combined. Beat in the vanilla, then add the eggs, one at a time, beating well after each addition until incorporated. On low speed, slowly add the flour mixture, continuing to beat until well mixed. Add the sour cream to the remaining chocolate mixture, stir well, and then pour into the egg-flour mixture and beat on medium speed until fully incorporated and the batter is smooth.

Pour the batter into the prepared Bundt pan, distributing it evenly. Bake the cake until a toothpick inserted near the center comes out with a few moist crumbs attached, 35–45 minutes. Be careful not to overbake or the cake will be dry. Let cool in the pan on a wire rack for 15–20 minutes, then loosen the cake sides from the pan (see Cook's Notes), invert the pan onto a wire rack, and lift off the pan. Let the cake cool completely.

GANACHE

6 oz (170 g) good-quality dark chocolate, finely chopped

¼ cup (60 ml) heavy cream

1½ tablespoons Irish whiskey

To make the ganache, put the chocolate into a heatproof bowl or a 2-cup (475-ml) glass measuring pitcher for easy pouring. In a small saucepan over medium heat, warm the cream just until it starts to steam and small bubbles appear along the edges of the pan. Pour the hot cream over the chocolate, let sit for 30 seconds, and then gently whisk, starting in the center and moving out in concentric circles until the chocolate is fully melted and smooth. Whisk in the whiskey, stirring until the mixture thickens slightly. It should be pourable but not so thin that it will all run down the sides of the cake.

Set the cooled cake still on the rack on a sheet pan (to catch any drips). Pour the warm ganache over top of the cake, letting it drizzle down the sides. Let set for a few minutes before slicing and serving.

COOK'S NOTES: Use a plastic knife to loosen the cake sides from the pan, running it up and down around the rim of the pan to ease the cake away from the sides without scratching the pan.

If you don't have nonstick baking spray with flour on hand, you can grease the pan well with vegetable oil or butter, making sure to reach every nook and cranny, and then dust the pan with flour, tapping out the excess.

CAFÉ DE OLLA
with Irish Liqueur

This traditional Mexican coffee tastes best when made in a Mexican *olla*, a wide-bottomed clay vessel with a fairly narrow neck. Preparing this classic in a pottery pot truly makes a difference, as the *olla* imparts a wonderful earthy quality to the drink. But if you don't have an *olla* or don't want to cook in *barro* (clay), this recipe can easily be made in a small stockpot or medium-large saucepan. Top off the finished coffee with a splash of Irish liqueur, such as Baileys, Irish Mist, or Sheridan's, for an authentic Saint Patrick's Day celebration.

MAKE 6 SERVINGS

6 cups (1.4 l) water

6–8 oz (170–225 g) piloncillo, chopped, or ¾–1 cup (155–210 g) packed dark brown sugar

2 cinnamon sticks

2 whole cloves

1 whole star anise pod

½ cup (40 g) freshly ground dark-roasted coffee

Irish liqueur, for serving

COOK'S NOTES: For a more authentic taste, Dark Mexican Coffee is recommended.

In a large olla or 3-quart (2.8-l) stockpot over high heat, bring the water to a boil. Carefully add the piloncillo, cinnamon sticks, cloves, and star anise and stir with a wooden spoon until the piloncillo dissolves, about 5 minutes. Add the coffee and stir to mix well, then reduce the heat to a simmer, cover, and simmer for 5 minutes.

Strain the coffee with a fine-mesh strainer into mugs, or strain into a large warmed container until ready to serve. Add a splash of liqueur to each mug before serving.

EASTER

Ever since I was a little girl, Easter has been one of my favorite holidays. It seems that as soon as Lent ends, the world is suddenly ablaze in color. The vivid shades of new spring growth are a welcome departure from the dark, chilly days of winter.

To celebrate this season of eternal rebirth, there's no better craft than *cascarones*, eggshells filled with multicolored paper confetti. I remember my mom would start saving eggshells as soon as Lent started. That would give us six weeks to start preparing for Easter. On the night before Easter Sunday, she would cover the table with newspaper and set out several glass bowls of water with color tablets, confetti, glue, and perfectly cut squares of tissue paper. We had so much fun making festive *cascarones*.

The next morning, we would gleefully run to find our Easter baskets, which would be filled with colorful grass, a chocolate bunny, Peeps (marshmallow chicks), and sometimes a small stuffed animal. Then we would dress up in our new Easter clothes to go to mass. Some years our mom even made our outfits, and those holidays were extra special. After mass, we would go back home and change into our play clothes for the yearly family barbecue and Easter egg hunt.

One of my *tías* (aunts) would host and the rest of the family would arrive with their *cascarones* and all the fixin's for a delicious spread: bowls of macaroni salad, brightly colored fruit salad, *chile con queso*, and guacamole, to name just a few of the offerings.

Finally, after everyone ate, it was time to hide the *cascarones*. The rest of the day was filled with giggles as my cousins and I hunted for the eggs and cracked them over friends' or family members' heads, raining down colorful confetti.

Our family's Easters continue to be large, casual, outdoor potluck-style celebrations, and my own children now know and enjoy all these traditions. Whether you're hosting a large Easter get-together like ours or an intimate gathering, I hope you'll try some of the recipes in this chapter, such as my Barbacoa de Borrego, fork-tender lamb in a red chile sauce, or my beautiful—and easy—Mango and Strawberry Galette. Or you might opt to host an Easter brunch featuring a hearty egg-topped hash of ham and sweet potato and a round of Bloody Marías for the grown-ups. However you choose to celebrate, I wish you *Felices Pasquas, mis amigos*!

Hacer de chivo los tamales

BARBACOA
de Borrego

Every region in Mexico has its own version of *barbacoa*, which is traditionally meat cooked—essentially steam-roasted—in an underground pit. It can be made from beef, goat, or lamb, typically the tougher cuts. In northern Mexico, it is sometimes made with beef head, including the cheeks. You can serve this lamb version as an elegant main dish on a fancy platter, casually as a filling for tacos or tamales, or as a topping on huevos rancheros (page 121) or chilaquiles (page 16) for brunch.

MAKES 8–12 SERVINGS

2 tablespoons vegetable oil

1 boneless lamb shoulder roast, 3½–4 lb (1.6–1.8 kg)

2 tablespoons tomato bouillon

CHILE COLORADO SAUCE

1 yellow onion, halved

3 tomatillos, husked, rinsed, and halved

2 tomatoes, halved

2 cloves garlic, peeled

4 guajillo chiles, stemmed

4 ancho or cascabel chiles, stemmed

1 cup (240 ml) water

2 tablespoons agave nectar

1 tablespoon cider vinegar

¼ teaspoon ground cinnamon

½ teaspoon dried Mexican oregano

1 teaspoon kosher salt

½ cup (120 ml) Mexican beer

Kosher salt

Chopped white onion and chopped fresh cilantro leaves, for garnish

In a very large frying pan over medium-high heat, warm the oil. Pat the lamb dry with a paper towel and sprinkle the bouillon on both sides. When the oil is hot, sear the lamb, turning as needed, until browned on all sides, about 5 minutes on each side. Transfer the meat to a slow cooker.

To make the sauce, return the pan with its drippings to medium-high heat. Add the onion, tomatillos, tomatoes, and garlic and roast, turning as needed, until lightly charred on both sides, about 7 minutes total. Transfer the onion, tomatillos, tomatoes, and garlic to a blender.

Return the pan to medium-low heat, add the guajillo and ancho chiles and heat, turning once, until lightly toasted, about 1 minute total. Transfer the chiles to a saucepan, add water to cover, bring to a boil over high heat, and boil until soft, about 15 minutes. Drain well and add to the blender.

Add the water, agave nectar, vinegar, cinnamon, oregano, and salt to the blender and purée until a smooth sauce forms. Transfer the sauce to the slow cooker. Then pour the beer into the slow cooker, distributing it evenly. Cover and cook on the low setting until fork-tender, about 8 hours.

Transfer the lamb to a cutting board and let rest for a few minutes to firm up, then coarsely shred the meat, discarding any bits of fat. Season to taste with salt.

To serve, spoon as much of the warm chile sauce as you like over the lamb, then garnish with the onion and cilantro.

HAM & SWEET POTATO
Hash

Hash, which is typically a chopped and fried mixture of meat, potatoes, and sometimes other vegetables, is a favorite way for American cooks to use up leftovers. I didn't grow up eating American-style hash, but this hash-inspired brunch main course reminds me of a dish my grandma and mom would make with leftover meat and potatoes. You can serve the hash homestyle, directly from the frying pan, or, for a more formal presentation, plate it in individual ramekins.

MAKES 4 SERVINGS

3 tablespoons olive oil

2 sweet potatoes, peeled and cut into ½-inch (12-mm) cubes

½ white onion, finely chopped

½ lb (225 g) ham steak, cut into ½-inch (12-mm) cubes

1 green bell pepper, seeded and chopped

1 jalapeño chile, diced

½ teaspoon red pepper flakes

¼ teaspoon ground black pepper

Kosher salt

1 cup (115 g) shredded Oaxaca or Muenster cheese (optional)

2 teaspoons butter

4 eggs

COOK'S NOTE: You can prepare the hash up to the point where it goes into the oven up to 2 days in advance, then cover and refrigerate. Proceed as directed, adding 5–10 minutes to the baking time.

Preheat the oven to 375°F (190°C).

Heat a large cast-iron frying pan over medium heat. When the pan is hot, add 2 tablespoons of the oil and swirl to coat the pan. Then add the sweet potatoes and fry, stirring frequently, until lightly browned, about 7 minutes.

Add the remaining 1 tablespoon oil to the pan along with the ham and continue to fry for 5 minutes. Add the bell pepper and jalapeño and fry until the bell pepper and jalapeño begin to soften, about 2 minutes more. Stir in the pepper flakes and black pepper and season with salt.

Spread the potato-ham mixture evenly in the pan and then, if using, sprinkle the cheese evenly over the top. Transfer the pan to the oven and bake for 10 minutes. If using the cheese, it should be melted and bubbling. If not using the cheese, the top should be lightly browned.

While the hash bakes, in a second large frying pan, melt the butter over medium heat. Carefully crack the eggs into the pan, reduce the heat to low, and fry until the whites are firm and the yolks have thickened, 3–4 minutes. Remove from the heat.

Remove the frying pan from the oven, top the hash with the eggs, and serve directly from the pan, or scoop the hash into medium-size ramekins and top each ramekin with an egg. Serve at once.

ENSALADA
de Coditos

This is the famous macaroni salad my mom makes for Easter and summer potlucks. As a child, it was a dish I looked forward to every year. I can still recall what it was like to scoop up a heaping spoonful onto my Styrofoam plate and eat every last bit of noodle. A meal in itself, this pasta dish is loaded with celery, green onion, black olives, pickles, cubes of cheese, and my mom's secret ingredient: Spam!

MAKES 12 SERVINGS

Salt

1 package (1 lb/450 g) elbow macaroni

1½ cups (350 ml) light mayonnaise

¼ cup (60 g) yellow mustard

3 celery ribs, thinly sliced

3 green onions, white and tender greens parts, sliced

½ cup (75 g) pitted black olives, chopped

½ cup (70 g) chopped dill or sour pickles

6 oz (170 g) Spam or ham, cut into ¼-inch (6-mm) dice

¼ lb (115 g) Muenster cheese, cut into ¼-inch (6-mm) cubes

½ lb (225 g) Colby cheese, cut into ¼-inch (6-mm) cubes

1 teaspoon ground black pepper

Bring a large pot of water to a boil and salt lightly. Add the macaroni and cook until al dente, according to package directions. Drain well but do not rinse. Transfer the macaroni to a large bowl, let cool for several minutes, and then cover with plastic wrap and refrigerate until cool.

In a small bowl, stir together the mayonnaise and mustard, mixing well. Add to the cooled macaroni, stirring lightly to coat evenly. Add the celery, green onions, olives, pickles, Spam, both cheeses, and pepper and stir until evenly distributed.

Cover and chill for at least 2 hours before serving to allow the flavors to blend. Serve cold.

 COOK'S NOTE: This creamy macaroni salad will keep in an airtight container in the refrigerator for up to 3 days.

SPRING FRUIT SALAD
with Tajín

I grew up in the 1980s and always remember a fluffy and sweet ambrosia-style fruit salad
made with canned fruit, Cool Whip, and shredded coconut. Don't get me wrong,
I loved that salad. But nowadays I would rather serve a bowl filled with colorful fresh fruits,
a scattering of crunchy jicama, a drizzle of lime juice, and a sprinkling of spicy Tajín.

For a festive touch, serve this salad in a hollowed-out pineapple or use a bunny-shaped
cookie cutter to cut some of the fruit pieces. You can also thread the fruit and jicama
pieces onto bamboo skewers for a great utensil-free potluck contribution.
If you are not a fan of papaya, replace it with cantaloupe.

MAKES 6–8 SERVINGS

1 small yellow mango, such
as Ataulfo, peeled, pitted, and
cubed

1 red-green mango, such as
a Haden, peeled, pitted, and
cubed

1 small jicama, peeled and
chopped

1 cup (170 g) chopped
pineapple

1 cup (140 g) chopped papaya

1 cup (155 g) watermelon, in
balls or cubes

1 teaspoon Tajín seasoning
(see Cook's Note)

Salt

3 tablespoons fresh lime juice

In a bowl, combine the mangos, jicama, pineapple, papaya, and
watermelon and toss gently to mix. Sprinkle with the Tajín,
season with salt, and drizzle with the lime juice, then toss well to
coat evenly.

Cover and refrigerate for at least 1 hour or for up to 1 day before
serving.

COOK'S NOTE: Tajín is a popular chile-salt-lime seasoning
mix made in Mexico and widely available in well-stocked
supermarkets and Latin stores in the United States. Clásico, the most
popular blend, is made with mild red chiles, while the habanero
blend delivers a lot more fire. A low-sodium version is also available.

MANGO AND
Strawberry Galette

My grandma made delicious empanadas and pies with the fruits—apple, apricot, peach, and *membrillo* (quince)—picked from trees in the backyard. When she had leftover dough, she would make an open-faced pie, with all the beautiful fruit exposed on the top. I now wonder if she was trying not to be wasteful or if she knew there was such a thing as a galette. The term *galette* is French for a free-formed tart. I love that this dessert is rustic, so it does not have to look perfect. It does not even require a pie dish to make it. The edges of the pastry are folded over the outer rim of the filling, leaving the center open, with the bright strawberries and exotic mangos visible. The boozy *dulce de leche*— thanks to orange liqueur—adds a touch of creamy richness at the table.

MAKES 6–8 SERVINGS

PASTRY

1¼ cups (155 g) all-purpose flour, plus more for dusting

2 teaspoons sugar

⅛ teaspoon salt

½ cup (115 g) cold unsalted butter, diced

1 large egg, lightly beaten

1–2 tablespoons cold water, if needed

FILLING

1½ cups (250 g) thinly sliced mango

1½ cups (250 g) sliced strawberries

2 tablespoons sugar

1 teaspoon pure vanilla extract

1 tablespoon cornstarch

1 large egg, lightly beaten, for the egg wash

Sugar, for sprinkling

To make the dough, in a good processor, combine the flour, sugar, and salt and pulse a few times to mix. Add the butter and pulse about ten times, until the butter is in pea-size pieces. Add the egg and pulse a few times, just until the mixture comes together in clumps. If the dough seems too dry, add the water, 1 tablespoon at a time, and pulse just until the dough holds together in a rough mass. Transfer the dough to a lightly floured work surface and shape into a thick disk. Wrap tightly in plastic wrap and refrigerate until firm, at least 1 hour or for up to overnight.

Position an oven rack in the lowest position in the oven and preheat the oven to 400°F (200°C). Line a sheet pan with parchment paper.

On a lightly floured work surface, roll out the dough into a round about 12 inches (30 cm) in diameter and ⅛ inch (3 mm) thick. Loosely wrap the dough around the rolling pin, then unroll it onto the prepared sheet pan, centering it on the pan.

To make the filling, in a bowl, combine the mango and strawberry slices, sugar, vanilla, and cornstarch and stir gently to coat the fruits evenly. Pour the fruit mixture onto the center of the dough round, leaving a 2-inch (5-cm) border uncovered. Fold the border up over the filling, forming loose pleats all around the edge and leaving the center open. Brush the edge of the dough with the egg wash, then, while the egg is still wet, lightly sprinkle the edge with sugar.

Bake the galette until the crust is golden brown and the filling is bubbly, about 30 minutes. Remove from the oven, then carefully

DULCE DE LECHE
ORANGE LIQUEUR

½ cup (150 g) dulce de leche

¼ cup (60 ml) orange liqueur

loosen with a wide metal spatula and slide onto a wire rack to cool slightly before serving.

While the galette is cooling, make the dulce de leche orange liqueur. In a heavy, small saucepan over low heat, combine the dulce de leche and liqueur and heat, stirring constantly, until hot. Remove from the heat.

Serve the galette warm, cut into wedges. Pass the dulce de leche orange liqueur at the table for guests to drizzle on top.

MINI CHEESE EMPANADAS
with Apricot-Jalapeño Jam

Zippy and versatile, this apricot-jalapeño jam goes wonderfully on a cream cheese–topped cracker. But it's even better as a filling in these dessert empanadas. You won't need all the filling for these empanadas, so you can experiment using it in other delicious ways, such as serving it as part of a charcuterie board.

Empanadas are one of those recipes that my son, Blake, loves to make with my mom, his *abuela*. He usually requests empanadas instead of a birthday cake. He loves to crimp their edges with a fork and brush the tops with sugar syrup. When I see their special bond, I am reminded of the bond I had at his age with my grandma.

MAKES 18 EMPANADAS

PASTRY

1½ cups (185 g) all-purpose flour, plus more for dusting

1 teaspoon baking powder

¼ teaspoon salt

¼ cup (60 g) solid vegetable shortening

1 tablespoon unsalted butter

1 large egg

¼ cup (60 ml) cold whole milk

1 teaspoon sugar

FILLING

1 jalapeño chile

1 cup (280 g) apricot preserves

½ lb (225 g) cream cheese

To make the pastry, in bowl, using an electric mixer, combine the flour, baking powder, and salt and beat on low speed for a few seconds to mix. Add the shortening and butter and beat on low speed just until the mixture forms large, coarse crumbs the size of peas. Add the egg, milk, and sugar and continue to beat on low speed until the dough comes together in a rough mass. Using your hands, gather the dough into a ball, flatten into a thick disk, wrap in plastic wrap, and refrigerate for 2 hours.

To make the filling, in a small saucepan over high heat, combine the jalapeño with water to cover and bring to a boil. Reduce the heat to medium and simmer the jalapeño until it softens, 10–12 minutes. Drain well, let cool until it can be handled, then remove the stem and seeds and chop finely. In a small bowl, combine the apricot preserves and jalapeño and mix well. Set aside.

To make the sugar syrup, in a second small saucepan over high heat, combine the water and sugar and bring to a boil, stirring until the sugar dissolves. Remove from the heat and let cool completely.

Position an oven rack in the center of the oven and a second rack in the top third of the oven and preheat the oven to 350°F (180°C). Spray a large sheet pan with cooking spray.

½ cup (120 ml) water

½ cup (100 g) sugar

Nonstick cooking spray, for the sheet pan

On a lightly floured work surface, roll out the pastry into a large round about ⅛ inch (3 mm) thick. Using a 3-inch (7.5-cm) round cookie cutter, cut out as many rounds as possible. Gather up the pastry scraps, press together, reroll, and cut out more rounds. You should have 18 rounds total.

To shape each empanada, place about a scant 1 tablespoon cream cheese and a small dollop of the apricot-jalapeño jam on half of a dough round. With a finger, dampen the edge of the round with water. Fold the uncovered half of the round over the filling to make a half-moon, pressing the edges together with your fingers and then sealing securely with the tines of a fork. Repeat until all the dough rounds are filled.

Arrange the empanadas on the prepared sheet pan, spacing them evenly. Lightly brush the top of each empanada with the sugar syrup and then puncture the top twice with fork tines (to allow steam to escape during baking). Place the pan on the center oven rack and bake the empanadas until golden brown, 15–20 minutes. If after 10 minutes, the bottoms are starting to brown too much, move the pan to the top oven rack for the final 5–10 minutes of baking. Let cool on the pan on a wire rack for at least a few minutes before serving. Serve warm or at room temperature. Store leftover empanadas in an airtight container at room temperature for up to 3 days.

MEXICAN SPRINKLE *Cookies*

These popular cookies are called *galletas de grageas* for their topping of small, round sprinkles in assorted colors. *Grageas* means "sprinkles," or, more specifically, the tiny, round rainbow sprinkles known as nonpareils, and I especially like using these decorations at Easter time because they remind me of the colorful confetti in *cascarones* (page 88). If you have ever visited a *panadería* (Mexican bakery), you are sure to have seen these colorful cookies. They have a crisp, crumbly exterior reminiscent of shortbread but a cakey interior, and they are known by other names as well, such as *galletas de chochitos* and *polvorones mexicanos*, depending on the region and the baker. They are extremely easy to make at home and are a fun baking project to do with kids.

MAKES EIGHTEEN 3-INCH (7.5-CM) COOKIES

1 cup (225 g) butter-flavored solid vegetable shortening

1 cup (200 g) sugar

⅛ teaspoon salt

1 large egg, plus 1 large egg, whisked, for the egg wash

2 teaspoons pure vanilla extract

2 cups (250 g) all-purpose flour, plus more for dusting

2 oz (60 g) rainbow nonpareils or other rainbow sprinkles (about 5 tablespoons)

Preheat the oven to 350°F (180°C). Have ready a large sheet pan.

In a bowl, using an electric mixer, beat the shortening on medium speed until light and fluffy. Add the sugar and salt and continue to beat on medium speed until smooth, about 1 minute. On low speed, add the egg and vanilla and beat until incorporated, 2–3 minutes.

Turn off the mixer, add about one-third of the flour, and then turn the mixer on low and beat until the flour is incorporated. Repeat with the remaining flour, adding one-third of the flour each time and always turning off the mixture before each addition.

When all the flour has been incorporated, turn the dough out onto a lightly floured work surface. Divide the dough into 4 equal portions and shape each portion into a ball. Cover and refrigerate 3 balls.

Roll out the fourth ball into a round ½ inch (12 mm) thick. Using a 3-inch (7.5-cm) round cookie cutter, cut out as many rounds as possible. Transfer the rounds to the sheet pan, spacing them 1 inch (2.5 cm) apart. Gather up the dough scraps and set aside. Repeat with the remaining dough balls, adding the cutouts to the pan. Press together all the dough scraps, reroll, and cut out more rounds. (You should be able to cut out 4 cookies per ball of dough with a 3-inch/7.5-cm cookie cutter. The dough scraps should yield a couple of more cookies.)

Brush the tops of the cookies with the egg wash, then sprinkle with the nonpareils. Bake the cookies until slightly browned, 10–12 minutes. Transfer the cookies to a wire rack and let cool for at least 10 minutes before serving. Serve warm or at room temperature. Store leftover cookies in an airtight container at room temperature for up to 5 days.

BLOODY MARÍA
with Serrano-Infused Tequila

Bloody Marys are a signature cocktail for an Easter brunch and are also a welcome Mother's Day drink. But why María and not Mary you ask? These Bloody Marías have swapped out the usual flavorless vodka for tequila blanco in which chiles have been steeped. For a large gathering, make a pitcher of the mix.

MAKES 1 SERVING

SPICY TEQUILA

2 serrano or jalapeño chiles

1 bottle (750 ml) tequila blanco

BLOODY MARÍA MIX

4 fl oz (120 ml) tomato juice

1 fl oz (30 ml) fresh lemon juice

Dash of Worcestershire sauce

Dash of Tabasco sauce

Kosher salt and freshly ground black pepper

Tajín (see Cook's Note, page 78) and lemon or lime wedge, for coating the glass rim (optional)

Ice cubes

Celery rib, fresh dill sprig, cherry tomatoes, lemon or lime slice or wedge, peperoncini, and/or pitted green olives, for garnish

To make the spicy tequila, stem the chiles (use jalapeños for a milder version) and cut lengthwise into thin strips. Add the chile strips to the bottle of tequila, cap the bottle tightly, and then shake the bottle gently. Let sit at room temperature overnight. The day of serving, strain the tequila through a fine-mesh sieve and discard the chile strips and seeds.

To make the Bloody María mix, in a measuring pitcher, stir together the tomato juice, lemon juice, and Worcestershire and Tabasco sauces. Season to taste with salt and pepper.

If desired, pour a little Tajín onto a small, flat plate. Run a lemon wedge around the rim of a tall glass, then roll the outer rim in the Tajín, coating it evenly.

Fill the glass with ice. Add the Bloody María mix and 2 fl oz (60 ml) of the spicy tequila and stir to mix. Garnish as you like with a celery rib, a dill sprig, a citrus slice or wedge, and/or speared cherry tomatoes, peperoncini, and olives.

Cascarones

Cascarones are empty eggshells that have been colored, filled with paper confetti, and sealed with colorful tissue paper. The name comes from the Spanish word *cáscara*, or "shell," and they regularly appear at Easter celebrations and fiestas, though they are a welcome addition at any festive occasion.

It wasn't until I left El Paso that I realized celebrating with *cascarones* is a Mexican tradition. I assumed every family made the confetti-filled eggshells and broke them over one another's heads on Easter Sunday. Imagine my embarrassment when I saw hard-boiled eggs hidden at an Easter party and asked, "Isn't it going to hurt when you break them on someone's head?"

Materials

Newspaper, craft paper, or a plastic tablecloth

Paper napkins or towel paper

Eggs

Easter egg coloring kit

Distilled white vinegar (optional)

Paper confetti or hole punched construction paper

Glue

Tissue paper, cut into very small squares

Prepare your work surface by covering it with newspaper. Be sure to have plenty of napkins handy for little decorators to dry their hands or for cleaning up any spills.

With a spoon, gently tap the top (the more pointed end) of an egg. Working carefully, remove the bits of shell, peeling away enough to make a hole about ½ inch (12 mm) in diameter. Empty the contents of the egg out into a bowl (the eggs can be used for custard, scrambled eggs, or whatever you like).

Using a gentle stream of water, thoroughly rinse the inside of the eggshell, then shake out any excess water. Let the eggshell air-dry upside down in an empty egg carton. Repeat to hollow out as many eggs as desired.

Following the instructions on the egg coloring kit, dye the eggshells. To ensure especially vibrant colors, add a splash of vinegar to each prepared dye bath. Let the eggshells dry completely on the kit tray, if provided, or on a wire rack.

When the eggshells are completely dry, fill each one with confetti. Apply glue around the outside of the hole in each shell and cover the hole with a square of tissue paper, pressing gently to adhere. Now you are ready to celebrate Easter.

CINCO
de Mayo

Did you know that Cinco de Mayo is actually a bigger deal in the United States than it is in Mexico? Contrary to what many believe, Cinco de Mayo is not Mexico's Independence Day (which is September 16; see page 170). Instead, it commemorates the 1862 Battle of Puebla, in which Mexican troops defeated the French (despite ultimately losing the war).

So why has it become such a cultural phenomenon in the United States? During the American Civil War in the 1860s, Mexican Americans celebrated Cinco de Mayo not only to promote cultural identity and solidarity but also to inspire the Latino troops who were fighting against Confederate forces. As the underdogs who were victorious against the forces of Napoleon III, the story of the Battle of Puebla was a beacon of hope for the Union Army.

When I was growing up, my family never celebrated Cinco de Mayo. In Mexico, it is more of a regional holiday that is mostly limited to Puebla. As a second-generation Mexican American with roots in Chihuahua, it was never a big piece of my identity. It wasn't until college that I discovered that celebrating Cinco de Mayo gave me an excellent excuse to share the music, food, and libations of my culture—to teach others about my Mexican heritage.

Nowadays, Cinco de Mayo is a festive occasion in our household, brimming with tasty and traditional Mexican dishes like my Tequila and Lime Carne Asada, Lamb Birria, and Cochinita Pibil with Spicy Pickled Onions. If you have a sweet tooth, you won't want to miss my baked churros topped with light, fluffy buttercream. And because no fiesta is complete without a great cocktail, I am also including my Jalapeño Mandarin Margarita.

I hope you'll take the opportunity to celebrate the beauty and resilience of Mexican culture with your amigos on Cinco de Mayo. String up some *papel picado*, cue up the mariachi music, and fire up the grill. When it comes to celebrating, always remember the more the merrier, regardless of your own heritage. *Salud* to Mexico, America, *familia*, and all that is *muy bueno*!

TEQUILA & LIME
Carne Asada

My carne asada marinade is super simple, requiring just a few easy-to-find ingredients.
The combination of butter, tequila, lime juice, lemon juice, garlic, serrano chile,
and fresh herbs not only packs the beef with flavor but also tenderizes it.
The alcohol in tequila acts much like natural fruit enzymes, breaking down the meat protein
for a more tender bite. Serve this carne asada sliced as a main with rice and vegetables
or for breakfast with eggs, or chop it as a filling for tacos.

MAKES 6–8 SERVINGS

4 tablespoons (60 g) butter, melted and cooled

¼ cup (60 ml) tequila reposado

Juice of 1 lemon

Juice of 1 lime

1 tablespoon chopped fresh thyme

1 serrano chile, finely chopped

3 cloves garlic, finely chopped

¼ cup (15 g) chopped fresh cilantro

½ cup (80 g) chopped red onion

1½ lb (680 g) flank, skirt, or flap steak

Kosher salt

In a small bowl, combine the butter, tequila, citrus juices, thyme, serrano, garlic, cilantro, and onion and mix well.

Put the steak into a large resealable plastic bag and pour in the marinade. Press the air out of the bag and seal it closed, then massage the marinade into the meat, distributing it evenly. (If you prefer, you can use a shallow dish, turning the steak to coat both sides well with the marinade and covering the dish with plastic wrap.) Let stand at room temperature for 30 minutes or in the refrigerator for up to 2 hours. If you refrigerate the steak, be sure to let it come to room temperature before grilling.

Prepare a fire in a charcoal or gas grill for direct grilling over high heat, or preheat a stove-top grill pan over high heat.

Remove the steak from the bag and season on both sides with salt. Grill the steak, turning once, for 5–7 minutes per side for medium-rare. The timing depends on the thickness of the steak. Transfer to a cutting board and let rest for 10 minutes.

To serve, cut the steak against the grain into slices ½ inch (12 mm) thick or chop it, depending on how you will be serving it.

COOK'S NOTES: Always let the meat rest before you slice or chop it. This allows the natural juices to redistribute evenly throughout the meat, ensuring a more succulent and tender result.

Tequila not only tenderizes the meat but also adds flavor. No tequila on hand? Replace it with beer or omit the alcohol.

COCHINITA PIBIL
with Spicy Pickled Onions

My husband, Bill, and I got married in the Mexican seaside town of Playa del Carmen, located on the northeastern coastline of the Yucatán Peninsula in an area known as the Riviera Maya. On my first trip there, I was excited to try the local cuisine. I had never heard of *cochinita pibil*, a specialty, but after just one bite, I knew I had to develop the recipe at home to transport me back to that memorable spot.

Cochinita pibil is spicy pulled pork that pops with the flavors of aromatic spices and citrus. The traditional marinade includes achiote, the seeds of the annatto tree, which are transformed into a seasoned paste that imparts a bright red-orange tinge and citrusy, earthy flavor to the pork. You can find achiote paste in Latin American markets or online.

Cochinita is "baby pig" in Spanish, and *pibil*, a Mayan word meaning "under the ground," refers to the cooking method developed by the Mayans. Traditionally, a whole pig is coated with the achiote seasoning paste, wrapped in banana leaves for added flavor, and then buried in a stone-lined pit with a fire at the bottom. If you don't have land in which you can dig a fire pit or readily available banana leaves, this easy but flavorful version of *cochinita pibil* prepared in a Dutch oven is for you.

———— ❧ • ❧ ————

MAKES 8–10 SERVINGS

COCHINITA PIBIL

1 tablespoon dried Mexican oregano

2 whole cloves

1 cinnamon stick

½ teaspoon black peppercorns

½ teaspoon cumin seeds

2 teaspoons coarse salt

¼ cup (80 g) achiote paste

6 cloves garlic, roughly chopped

Continues on the following page

To make the cochinita pibil, put the oregano, cloves, cinnamon, peppercorns, cumin, and salt into a mortar and crush with a pestle until pulverized. Set aside.

In a blender, combine the achiote paste, garlic, orange and lime juices, half of the onion, and the pulverized spices and blend until puréed to make a marinade.

Put the meat into a glass container and pour the marinade over the meat. Turn and massage the meat until it is well covered with the marinade. Cut the remaining onion into slices and arrange the onion slices and bay leaves on top of the meat. Cover and let stand at room temperature for 30 minutes or refrigerate for up to overnight.

Preheat the oven to 325°F (165°C).

Continued from the previous page

Juice of 3 large oranges

Juice of 2 limes

½ red onion, halved

1 bone-in pork shoulder roast, 4 lb (1.8 kg), cut into 4-inch (10-cm) pieces

2 bay leaves

SPICY PICKLED ONIONS

2 large red onions, sliced into rings ⅛ inch (3 mm) thick

3 habanero chiles, sliced

½ cup (120 ml) fresh lime juice (from 3–4 limes)

⅔ cup (160 ml) fresh orange juice (from 1–2 oranges)

1½ teaspoons salt

Corn tortillas, warmed, for serving

Remove the meat and the marinade from the glass container and place it in a Dutch oven. Cover and bake until the meat is very tender, about 3 hours. It should fall apart easily when pulled with a fork. If not, return the pot to the oven and continue to bake for 15 minutes or so and test again.

While the pork is cooking, make the pickled onions. Bring a kettle of water to a boil. Put the onions into a heatproof glass or ceramic bowl, add boiling water to cover, and let stand for 1 minute. Drain the onions into a colander. Return the onions to the bowl, add the habaneros, citrus juices, and salt, and stir and toss to mix well. Cover and set aside until serving time.

When the pork is ready, using 2 forks or your fingers, shred the meat and pile it on a platter. Serve with the tortillas and pickled onions and eat taco style.

 COOK'S NOTE: The recipe can be cooked in a slow cooker on the low setting for 6–8 hours.

VARIATION: This is a good way to use up leftover Thanksgiving turkey. Omit the pork. Make the marinade as directed. In a saucepan, combine the marinade and 3 cups (450 g) shredded cooked turkey and cook uncovered over medium-low heat until the meat has absorbed most of the marinade, about 5 minutes. The dish should be very moist but not soupy.

LAMB
Birria

Try this authentic Mexican recipe that can be eaten as a classic old-world stew or as trendy cheesy *quesabirria* tacos dipped in a side of consommé. Consommé is the cooking liquid that results after slowly cooking the meat in water seasoned with onion, garlic, and herbs and then mixing the broth with red chile sauce. Birria originated in the state of Jalisco, where it is traditionally made with goat or lamb. Feel free to use beef for a more affordable and easier-to-find option.

MAKES 6–8 SERVINGS

BIRRIA

8 cups (1.9 l) water

1 boneless leg of lamb, about 4 lb (1.8 kg), trimmed of excess fat and cut into 4-inch (10-cm) cubes

½ white onion

8 cloves garlic, peeled

1 tablespoon salt

1½ teaspoons black peppercorns

3 bay leaves

½ teaspoon dried Mexican oregano

2 fresh marjoram sprigs

2 fresh thyme sprigs (optional)

1 fresh mint sprig

Salt and ground black pepper

Continues on the following page

To make the birria, in a slow cooker, combine the water, lamb, onion, garlic, salt, peppercorns, bay leaves, oregano, marjoram, thyme (if using), and mint. Cover and cook on the low setting for 8–10 hours. The meat should be very tender.

Transfer the meat to a cutting board and let sit for a few minutes to firm up, then, using 2 forks or your fingers, shred the meat, discarding any bits of fat. Taste and adjust the seasoning with salt and pepper if needed, then return the meat to the broth in the slow cooker.

While the meat is cooking, make the chile sauce. Stem, seed, and devein the guajillo and ancho chiles, put them into a colander, and rinse well under cold running water. Transfer the chiles to a saucepan, add the garlic, onion, water, and salt, and bring to a boil over high heat. Reduce the heat to medium, cover, and simmer, turning the chiles over after about 10 minutes to ensure they cook evenly, until the chiles have softened, about 20 minutes.

Remove from the heat and let cool, then transfer the contents of the pan to a blender and blend until smooth. Strain the sauce through a fine-mesh sieve into the slow cooker with the meat and broth and stir to mix well. The broth combined with the red sauce is the "consommé." Discard the skins and seeds in the sieve.

To serve the birria as a stew, reheat the lamb and consommé to serving temperature, then spoon into individual bowls and garnish with the onion, radishes, and cilantro. Serve with the lime wedges and tortillas.

Continued from the previous page

RED CHILE SAUCE

8 guajillo or New Mexico chiles

2 ancho chiles (optional)

3 cloves garlic, peeled

¼ white onion

5 cups (1.2 l) water

2 teaspoons salt

FOR STEW

Chopped white onion, chopped or sliced radishes, and chopped fresh cilantro, for garnish

Lime wedges

Corn tortillas, warmed

FOR TACOS

Yellow corn tortillas

Shredded Chihuahua, Oaxaca, or Monterey jack cheese

Chopped white onion and chopped fresh cilantro, for garnish

Lime wedges

To serve the birria in quesabirria tacos, preheat the oven to 200°F (95°C). Have ready a large sheet pan. Scoop the lamb out of the consommé and set aside in a bowl; keep warm. Heat a comal (cast-iron griddle) or frying pan over medium-low heat. One at a time, dip a tortilla into the consommé and place on the comal. Top the tortilla with a layer of cheese. Arrange some shredded lamb over half of the tortilla, top the lamb with onion and cilantro, and drizzle the meat with a little more consommé. Wait until the cheese melts, then fold the tortilla in half and cook, flipping the taco over once the underside is browned, until browned and slightly crispy on both sides, 2–3 minutes on each side. Transfer the taco to the sheet pan and keep warm in the oven. Repeat until all the tacos are assembled.

Top the tacos with additional onion and cilantro, then serve with the lime wedges and with small bowls of warm consommé for dipping.

COOK'S NOTES: Beef can be used in place of the lamb. Use boneless beef chuck roast or beef shank. If you don't have a slow cooker or just want to speed up the cooking, the birria can be cooked in a covered Dutch oven in a preheated 325°F (165°C) oven for about 3 hours.

The red chile sauce can be made in advance and kept in an airtight container in the refrigerator for up to 1 week or in the freezer for up to 6 months.

As with most soups and stews, birria can be made a day in advance and stored in the refrigerator, then simply reheated before serving. Any leftovers will keep in an airtight container in the refrigerator for up to 1 week or in the freezer for up to 3 months.

GUACAMOLE
with Pomegranate

I like nearly every guacamole. The only ones I don't like are the commercial ones that contain artificial stuff and are full of tangy preservatives. If guacamole is made with perfectly ripe Hass avocados from Mexico, sign me up. This simple and unique guacamole is jeweled with ruby-red pomegranate seeds.

— ❦ • ❧ —

MAKES 12 SERVINGS

4 large avocados

2 green onions, white and pale green parts, sliced

1 jalapeño chile, minced (optional)

3 tablespoons chopped fresh cilantro

1½ teaspoons salt

1–2 tablespoon fresh lime juice

Pomegranate seeds, for garnish

Tortilla chips, for serving

Halve and pit the avocados, then scoop the flesh from the skin into a bowl. Using a fork, mash the avocado flesh, leaving it a bit chunky.

Add the onions, jalapeño (if using), cilantro, and salt to the bowl, then sprinkle 1 tablespoon of the lime juice over all the ingredients. Give everything a good stir, but don't overdo it. Taste and adjust the seasoning with salt and more lime juice if needed.

Top with a scattering of pomegranate seeds and serve with tortilla chips.

COOK'S NOTE: I like the ingredients in these proportions, but you can add more or less of each ingredient as you like to satisfy your own palate. Avocado flesh oxidizes (turns brown) fairly quickly when exposed to oxygen. Prep any of the other ingredients earlier in the day, but leave the avocado mashing until the last minute.

VARIATION: If you own a molcajete and tejolote—lava-stone mortar and pestle—combine the onions, jalapeño, and salt in the mortar and grind together with the pestle until a paste forms. Halve, pit, peel, and dice the avocados and fold them into the onion-chile paste, keeping the diced avocado fairly intact. Sprinkle 1 tablespoon of the lime juice over the top and stir gently just until mixed, keeping the mixture chunky. Taste and adjust the seasoning with salt and more lime juice if needed. Top with the pomegranate seeds and serve immediately directly from the mortar. Accompany with tortilla chips.

JALAPEÑO MANDARIN
Margarita

I love a margarita made from scratch rather than from a commercial mixer, and this simple margarita made with tequila reposado, fresh citrus juice, orange liqueur, charred lime, and jalapeño is a match made in cocktail heaven. I am all about spicy and smoky drinks, and while this drink is smoky, it is also very refreshing. If you enjoy the flavor of smoky cocktails, try this cocktail with mezcal instead of tequila.

MAKES 2 COCKTAILS

Tajín (see Cook's Note, page 78) and lemon or lime wedge, for coating the glass rim

1 lime, halved

½ jalapeño chile, seeded

4 fl oz (120 ml) tequila reposado or mezcal

2 fl oz (60 ml) orange liqueur

Juice of 1 lime juice

Juice of 2 mandarin oranges

Ice cubes

Mandarin orange and jalapeño slices, for garnish

Pour a little Tajín onto a small, flat plate. Run the lime wedge around the rim of a short tumbler, then roll the outer rim in the Tajín, coating it evenly. Repeat with a second tumbler and set the glasses aside.

On a stove-top grill pan over medium-high heat, char the lime halves, turning as needed, until lightly charred on all sides, 5–8 minutes. Transfer the lime halves to a cocktail shaker.

Add the jalapeño to the lime and, using a muddler or a wooden spoon, muddle them to release their juices. Add the tequila, orange liqueur, lime juice, and mandarin juice and fill the shaker two-thirds-full with ice. Cover and shake vigorously until the outside of the shaker is lightly frosted.

Fill the prepared glasses with ice. Strain the margarita mixture into the glasses, dividing it evenly. Garnish with mandarin and jalapeño slices and serve.

BAKED CHURROS
with Lavender-Lemon Buttercream

These baked churros are crisp and coated with cinnamon sugar on the outside, pillowy soft on the inside, and piled high with lavender-lemon buttercream. This is the ultimate dessert to celebrate Cinco de Mayo or Mexican Independence Day.

MAKES ABOUT 24 SMALL ROUND CHURROS

CINNAMON SUGAR

½ cup (100 g) granulated sugar

½ teaspoon ground cinnamon

CHURROS

2 cups (475 ml) water

5 tablespoons plus 1 teaspoon (80 g) unsalted butter

2 tablespoons packed light brown sugar

½ teaspoon salt

2 cups (250 g) all-purpose flour

4 large eggs

1 teaspoon pure vanilla extract

Nonstick cooking spray, for coating the churros

Preheat the oven to 375°F (190°C). Line 2 sheet pans with parchment paper.

To make the cinnamon sugar, in a small, shallow bowl, stir together the granulated sugar and cinnamon. Set aside.

To make the churros, in a heavy saucepan over medium heat, combine the water, butter, brown sugar, and salt and bring to a full boil. Add the flour all at once and stir vigorously with a wooden spoon. Continue to stir until a film forms on the bottom of the pan and the mixture pulls away from the sides of the pan and forms a ball, 1–2 minutes. Remove from the heat and transfer the mixture to the bowl of a stand mixer fitted with the paddle attachment.

Beat on medium-low speed until there is no more visible steam, at least 5 minutes. Add the eggs, one at a time, beating well after each addition until the mixture is once again smooth. You can do this all with a sturdy wooden spoon instead of a mixer, but the mixture is thick and tiring to mix by hand. Either way, continue mixing until the batter is smooth, then beat in the vanilla.

Fit a piping bag with an open star tip about ½ inch (12 mm) in diameter (a closed star will also work.) The star tip creates the distinctive churro ridges. Fill the bag with the batter (stand it tip down in a tall drinking glass to simplify filling) and twist the top closed. Pipe the batter into 2½-inch (6-cm) spirals onto the prepared pans, spacing them about 2 inches (5 cm) apart. Dampen a fingertip with water and gently flatten the top seam on each spiral.

LAVENDER-LEMON BUTTERCREAM

1–2 tablespoons dried culinary lavender buds

1½ tablespoons hot water

Grated zest and juice of 1 large lemon

3 cups (340 g) confectioners' sugar

5 tablespoons (75 g) cold unsalted butter, cut into chunks

½ teaspoon pure lemon extract (optional; for a stronger lemon flavor)

Bake the churros until lightly browned, 35–45 minutes. Remove from the oven, then immediately spray the tops lightly with cooking spray, dunk each top into the cinnamon sugar to coat lightly, and set right side up on a wire rack. Let cool completely. The churros are best eaten the day they are baked, but they will keep in an airtight container at room temperature for up to 3 days.

While the churros are baking, make the buttercream. In a small bowl, combine the lavender and hot water and let steep for 10 minutes. Transfer the steeped lavender and its water to a food processor along with the lemon zest, confectioners' sugar, butter, and 1 tablespoon of the lemon juice and process until smooth and creamy, stopping to scrape down the sides of the processor as needed. Add up to 1 tablespoon more lemon juice to achieve a good consistency, then taste and add the lemon extract if a stronger lemon flavor is desired. Transfer to a bowl, cover, and refrigerate for at least 30 minutes before using.

To serve the churros, spoon or pipe the buttercream onto the tops of the cooled churros, or top half of the churros with buttercream and place a second churro on top to form a churro sandwich.

Papel Picado

You can either make your own *papel picado*—paper flags with intricate cutout patterns—for your fiesta or you can purchase the flags. I highly recommend mesachicparties.com for all your fiesta supply needs.

Mini Piñatas

Skip the favor bags and make these tiny, colorful piñatas instead.

For each piñata, tape a loop of ribbon to use for hanging to the top of a bathroom-tissue tube. Cut a ¾-inch (2-cm) X in the center of a 2½-inch (6-cm) square of tissue paper. Glue the square over the bottom of the tube.

Cut colored tissue paper into strips 1½ inches (4 cm) wide and at least 6½ inches (16.5 cm) long (to speed the task, fold the tissue paper to cut many strips at once). Cut fringe 1 inch (2.5 cm) long and about ¼ inch (6 mm) wide along the length of each strip. Starting at the bottom of the tissue tube, wrap a strip, fringe edge down, around the tube, securing it in place with glue. Continue to wrap strips around the tube, layering them to expose about ½ inch (12 mm) of the previous strip and gluing them in place, until the entire tube is covered with strips.

Tape a length of ribbon across the X on the tissue paper covering the bottom of the tube. Fill the tube with paper confetti and hang it up, using the ribbon taped to the top.

Invite guests to pull the bottom ribbon on each piñata to release the colorful surprise.

MOTHER'S
Day

Here in the United States, Mother's Day is celebrated every second Sunday of May. In Mexico, Mother's Day always falls on May 10. Depending on the year, Mexican American families will often have two separate celebrations to show thanks for their moms. That may seem over the top to some people, but moms are prized in Mexican culture.

Although Mexico is primarily a patriarchal society with strong elements of machismo, the importance of mothers is universally recognized. This high regard for motherhood can be traced back centuries. Our Lady of Guadalupe (aka the Virgin Mary) is widely considered to be the patron saint of Latin America. Although Our Lady's popularity was originally rooted in Catholicism, the Virgin Mother is now seen as a strong symbol of Mexican identity that reaches beyond religion—a figure who is often used to represent social justice movements. In essence, Our Lady is the Mother of Mexico, and as a result, reverence for her and all mothers extends to every corner of the country.

All of this makes Mother's Day an especially significant holiday for Latinos. When I recall the holiday, I get teary-eyed thinking of the two most important women in my life, my mother and my late grandma Jesusita. These two women raised me to become the woman, cook, and mother that I am today, and I am forever grateful.

Some of my fondest memories are of being with them in the kitchen, so I do my best to honor these two matriarchs by continuing the tradition of cooking Mexican food for my loved ones. *Muy Bueno Fiestas* would not exist without their motherly influence!

Mother's Day is the perfect time to celebrate *las reinas de la casa* (queens of the home) with food, gifts, and festivities. As a mother myself, I find that there is no more universal love language than homemade food. I encourage you to treat the mothers in your life to a delicious brunch (or breakfast in bed!) with any of these special recipes.

If your special lady has a sweet tooth, try starting off her day with French toast topped with a raisin-laced *piloncillo* syrup or with streusel-layered coffee cake. If she favors the savory side of the menu, make Huevos Rancheros or Tampiqueña Steak. Whether you go sweet or savory, be sure to toast her motherly excellence with some deliciously tropical Guava Mimosas and to tell her, *"Eres la mejor mamá y te amo,"* so she knows she's the best.

Caras vemos, corazones no conocemos

MEXICAN
Coffee Cake

Cafecito y Chisme—"coffee and gossip"—are a tradition in Mexico.
When my mom and I sit down with a *cafecito*, we always catch up on all the family news.
This cake is best served with a cup of coffee and some spicy gossip.

MAKES 12 SERVINGS

Nonstick baking spray with flour, for the pan

3 cups (375 g) all-purpose flour

1 teaspoon salt

1 teaspoon baking soda

2 teaspoons instant coffee powder

¼ teaspoon ground cloves

1 cup (225 g) unsalted butter, at room temperature

2 cups (400 g) granulated sugar

1 tablespoon pure vanilla extract

4 large eggs, at room temperature

2 cups (450 g) sour cream, at room temperature

2 teaspoons instant coffee powder dissolved in ¼ cup (60 ml) boiling water, then cooled

Preheat the oven to 350°F (180°C). Spray a 10-inch (25-cm) tube pan with baking spray.

In a medium bowl, whisk together the flour, salt, baking soda, coffee powder, and cloves. In a large bowl, using an electric mixer, beat together the butter and granulated sugar on medium-high speed until light in color and fluffy, about 4 minutes. On low speed, add the vanilla and then add the eggs, one at a time, beating well after each addition. Add the flour mixture in three batches alternately with the sour cream in two batches, beginning and ending with the flour mixture and beating after each addition just until mixed. Add the cooled coffee and beat until combined.

To make the streusel, in a small bowl, stir together the brown sugar, nuts, and cinnamon, mixing well.

Spoon one-third of the batter into the prepared tube pan. Sprinkle one-third of the streusel over the batter. Repeat the batter and streusel layers twice.

Bake the cake until a toothpick inserted near the center comes out clean, 60–65 minutes. Let cool in the pan on a wire rack for 10 minutes, then, using a knife, loosen the cake sides from the pan (use a plastic knife to avoid scratching the pan), invert the pan onto a wire rack, and lift off the pan. Let the cake cool completely.

STREUSEL

¾ cup (155 g) packed dark
brown sugar

¾ cup (90 g) chopped walnuts
or pecans

2 tablespoons ground
cinnamon

COFFEE GLAZE

2 cups (225 g) confectioners'
sugar

2–3 tablespoons strong brewed
coffee, at room temperature

To make the glaze, in a bowl, whisk together the confectioners' sugar
and 2 tablespoons of the coffee until smooth, adding additional coffee
if needed for a good fluid glaze consistency.

Set the cake still on the rack on a sheet pan to catch any drips and
drizzle the glaze over the top, allowing it to drip down the sides. Let
set for a few minutes before serving.

CABALLEROS *Pobres*

Caballeros pobres, which roughly translates to "poor knights" or "poor gentlemen," is a decadent Yucatan dish of bread soaked in an egg-and-milk mixture and then panfried. Think of it as the Mexican version of French toast. My version is similar in flavor to one of my favorite desserts, *capirotada* (page 30), but instead of using *bolillo*s for the bread, I use thick, fluffy challah. The traditional recipe calls for dipping the bread into an egg-white meringue and then frying the slices. In my simplified version, I use whole eggs and bake the slices to cut down on prep time.

MAKES 6–12 SERVINGS

FRENCH TOAST

6 large eggs

1 cup (240 ml) whole milk

1 cup (240 ml) buttermilk

1 tablespoon pure vanilla extract

½ teaspoon ground cinnamon

¼ teaspoon coarse salt

Nonstick cooking spray, for the baking dish and foil

12 slices day-old challah, brioche, or French bread, about ¾ inch (2 cm) thick

PILONCILLO-RAISIN SYRUP

1 cup (240 ml) water

6 oz (170 g) piloncillo, chopped, or 1 cup (210 g) packed dark brown sugar

2 tablespoons fresh orange juice

1 cinnamon stick

4 whole cloves

⅓ cup (60 g) golden raisins

Toasted pecan halves and grated orange zest, for garnish

To make the French toast, in a bowl, whisk the eggs until blended. Whisk in the milk, buttermilk, vanilla, cinnamon, and salt, mixing well.

Spray the bottom and sides of a 9 x 13-inch (23 x 33-cm) baking dish with cooking spray. Working in batches, dip the bread slices into the egg mixture, coating them well, then arrange them in the baking dish in a single layer, overlapping the slices. Pour any remaining egg mixture evenly over the top. Cover and refrigerate for at least 2 hours or for up to overnight.

Preheat the oven to 375°F (190°C).

Remove the baking dish from the refrigerator. Spray a sheet of aluminum foil large enough to cover the baking dish with cooking spray and cover the dish, sprayed side down. Bake for 25 minutes. Uncover the dish and continue to bake until the top is golden brown and crunchy, 20–25 minutes longer.

While the toast is baking, make the syrup. In a heavy saucepan over medium-high heat, combine the water, piloncillo, orange juice, cinnamon, and cloves and bring to a boil, stirring to dissolve the piloncillo. Reduce the heat to a simmer and simmer uncovered, stirring occasionally, until a syrup forms, about 5 minutes. Remove from the heat and set aside to steep for 30 minutes. Pour through a fine-mesh sieve into a serving pitcher or bowl and discard the cinnamon sticks and cloves. Add the raisins, stir to mix, and set aside until serving.

When the French toast is ready, remove from the oven. Transfer the slices to individual plates, sprinkle with the pecans and orange zest, and serve. Pass the syrup at the table.

GORDITAS
de Picadillo

In most of Mexico, *gorditas* are corn pockets, similar to a pita or *arepa*, made from masa harina (corn flour) and shaped like a tortilla but thicker. (In northern Mexico, they are made from wheat flour.) Our family's secret ingredient is the addition of mashed potato to the corn dough. Crisp on the outside and soft on the inside, these tasty pockets can be filled with almost anything you have on hand. In El Paso, the most common filling at fiestas or bazaars is *picadillo* (ground beef and potato).

My grandma used to make delicious *gorditas* de *picadillo* for us at home and also for the annual bazaar at our local Catholic church. She would help at the church bazaar for hours, which she did up to the age of ninety. My mom now volunteers and makes *gorditas* at the church. The long lines at the *gorditas* booth are a testament to their popularity. Everyone knows they are special and worth the wait.

MAKES 8 GORDITAS

PICADILLO

1 large russet potato, peeled and diced

2 teaspoons salt

1 lb (450 g) ground beef

¼ cup (40 g) chopped white onion

1 teaspoon garlic powder

1 teaspoon ground black pepper

Continues on the following page

To make the picadillo, in a saucepan over medium-high heat, combine the potato, 1 teaspoon of the salt, and water to cover, bring to a boil, and boil until the potato is tender, about 10 minutes. Drain and set aside.

In a dry frying pan over medium heat, cook the beef, breaking up the meat and stirring often, until browned, about 10 minutes. Using a potato masher, gently mash the meat so no large chunks remain. Add the onion and cook, stirring occasionally, until translucent, about 2 minutes. Reduce the heat to low, add the remaining 1 teaspoon salt, the garlic powder, pepper, and cooked potato, and cook, stirring occasionally, to blend the flavors, about 3 minutes. Taste and adjust the seasoning with salt if needed. If the picadillo is too dry, add 1–2 tablespoons water. Remove from the heat and keep warm.

To make the gorditas, in a saucepan over medium-high heat, combine the potato, ¾ teaspoon of the salt, and water to cover, bring to a boil, and boil until the potato is soft enough to mash, about 15 minutes. Drain, mash, and measure 1 cup (325 g) for the dough. Reserve any remaining potato for another use.

In a large bowl, stir together the masa harina, warm water, the remaining ¼ teaspoon salt, and the mashed potato, mixing well. Knead in the bowl until moist and soft, about 5 minutes. Cover the bowl with a kitchen towel and let the dough stand for about 15 minutes.

Continued from the previous page

GORDITAS

1 small russet potato, peeled and cubed

1 teaspoon salt

2 cups (230 g) masa harina (corn flour)

1½ cups (350 ml) warm water

Canola oil, for deep-frying

Shredded lettuce, chopped tomato, shredded cheese, and/or salsa, for topping (see Cook's Note)

Divide the dough into 8 equal portions. Using your hands, shape each portion into a patty about ¼ inch (6 mm) thick.

Line a large plate with paper towels and set it near the stove. Pour the oil to a depth of 4 inches (10 cm) into a wide, heavy saucepan or wok and heat over high heat until very hot. Gently drop 2 or 3 patties into the oil. They will sink to the bottom of the pan. When they rise to the surface, after 3–5 minutes, turn them over and allow to cook for another 2–3 minutes. They are ready when they are a uniform golden brown. Using tongs or a slotted spoon, transfer them to the towel-lined plate to drain. Cook the remaining dough patties the same way.

Let the gorditas cool slightly, about 2 minutes. Then, using a small serrated knife, carefully slit the edge open along half of each gordita to create a pocket. Stuff the pockets with the picadillo and your toppings of choice and serve warm.

COOK'S NOTE: The toppings can be varied according to taste. Iceberg lettuce, Longhorn Colby cheese, and Salsa de Molcajete (page 165) are all good choices.

GRIDDLE VARIATION: You can cook the gorditas on a griddle instead of fry them. Lightly oil a large stove-top griddle or cast-iron frying pan and heat over medium heat. Cook each gordita, turning once, until the center slightly puffs up and both sides are browned in spots, 3–4 minutes on each side.

HUEVOS *Rancheros*

This recipe (literally "ranchers' eggs") is a typical Mexican breakfast featuring lightly fried corn tortillas topped with refried beans, fried eggs, and plenty of salsa. It was traditionally served to ranchers as a late-morning breakfast after they had been hard at work, so you know it's hearty and delicious!

MAKES 2–4 SERVINGS

2 tablespoons canola oil

4 corn tortillas

1 tablespoon olive oil

2 cups (475 ml) Salsa de Molcajete (page 165)

1 cup (240 ml) vegetable broth

2 cups (520 g) refried beans, warmed

4 large eggs, cooked any style (sunny-side up is recommended)

Crumbled queso fresco, for garnish (optional)

Line a large plate with paper towels and set it near the stove. In a heavy frying pan over high heat, warm the canola oil. When the oil is hot, add the tortillas, one at a time, and fry, turning once, until lightly crisp and golden, 20–40 seconds on each side. Transfer to the towel-lined plate to drain.

In a saucepan over medium heat, warm the olive oil. Add the salsa and cook, stirring often, for 3 minutes. Add the broth, stir well, and bring to a simmer. Cook, stirring occasionally, until most of the liquid has been absorbed, 7–10 minutes.

Just before the salsa is ready, spoon the beans into a microwave-safe bowl and microwave on high power for 25-second intervals, stirring after each interval, until hot, about 1 minute. Alternatively, warm on the stove top over medium-low heat, stirring often, until hot.

To assemble each serving, place 1–2 fried tortillas (tostadas) on an individual plate; spoon on one-fourth of the beans atop each tortilla, top with an egg and then the salsa, and sprinkle with the queso fresco, if using. Serve at once.

TAMPIQUEÑA
Steak

The word *tampiqueña* refers to a Mexican style of cooking steak that originated at the Tampico Club in Mexico City in 1939. The steak—traditionally *arrachera*, or "skirt steak"—is seasoned with salt and pepper, grilled, and then topped with caramelized onions, roasted green chiles, and shredded cheese and broiled until all the toppings are piping hot and the cheese is melted. The chiles add a lively flavor, and the cheese complements the meat. It can be served as a whole steak or *a la mexicana*, which calls for cubing the grilled steak before the toppings are added. I secretly call this latter version *a la mamá* because it's as if your mom cut your beef for you.

If this dish is on a restaurant's menu, I usually order it. I can't resist it! In El Paso, it is typically served with a red cheese enchilada, Mexican rice, refried beans, and chunky guacamole.

MAKES 4 SERVINGS

3 tablespoons butter

2 white onions, sliced

4 fresh Anaheim or Hatch chiles, roasted, peeled, seeded, and cut lengthwise into strips 1 inch (2.5 cm) wide (page 15)

1 lb (450 g) skirt steak

Kosher salt and freshly ground black pepper

1 cup (115 g) shredded Oaxaca or asadero cheese

COOK'S NOTE: Feel free to omit the cheese.

In a large frying pan over medium-low heat, melt the butter. When the butter foams, add the onions and cook, stirring occasionally, until translucent and starting to brown lightly, 12–14 minutes. Add the chile strips and cook, stirring, for 2–3 minutes to mix well. Remove from the heat and set aside.

Prepare a fire in a charcoal or gas grill for direct grilling over medium-high heat. Preheat the broiler.

Season the steak on both sides with salt and pepper and cut into 4 equal servings. Line a sheet pan with aluminum foil.

Place the steak on the grill, close the lid, and grill, turning once, for 2–3 minutes on each side for medium-rare to medium, or cook to your desired doneness. Transfer the steak to the foil-lined sheet pan and let rest for 2 minutes. If you want to serve the steak a la mexicana, transfer the steak to a cutting board, chop it, and then return it to the sheet pan.

Top the steak with the onion and chile mixture and sprinkle with the cheese. Place under the broiler and broil until the cheese melts and bubbles, 1–2 minutes. Serve at once.

Cada quien tiene su sazón

FRESH FRUIT CUPS
with Chamoy & Tajín

One of my favorite snacks from street-food vendors in Mexico are fruit cups. I love passing by the carts and seeing all the colorful fruits, and then watching the vendor cut the fruits in front of the customers and serve them. There is nothing fresher, and that screams Mexico louder, than fresh fruits with spicy Tajín powder and sticky and tangy chamoy sauce. Feel free to choose your favorite fruits for the cups.

MAKE 8 SERVINGS

1 small seedless watermelon, peeled

2 English cucumbers, peeled

1 jicama, peeled

2 mangos, peeled and pitted

1 small papaya, halved, seeded, and peeled

1 pineapple, peeled and cored

2 limes

Tajín, for seasoning (see Cook's Note, page 78)

Chamoy sauce, for serving (optional; see Cook's Note)

Cut the watermelon, cucumbers, jicama, mangos, papaya, and pineapple into large spears. Stand the spears in 8 cups or glasses, dividing the various fruits evenly among the cups (use disposable plastic cups for an authentic street-food touch).

Quarter the limes and squeeze the juice over the fruits in the cups. Sprinkle the fruits with Tajín, drizzle with the chamoy sauce, if using, and serve.

COOK'S NOTE: Chamoy sauce is a thick syrup made from lime, chile, and fruit, such as apricots, mangos, and/or plums. It is sold in bottles in Latin markets and online.

GUAVA
Mimosas

No Mother's Day breakfast or brunch is complete without a beautiful mimosa. Guavas are highly aromatic, with a flavor between pear and strawberry, and a batch of these mimosas will bring a whole new floral and sweet profile to your holiday table.

MAKES 6 SERVINGS

2 cups (475 ml) water

4 ripe guavas, chopped

3 tablespoons agave nectar

1 bottle (750 ml) cava, Champagne, or sparkling white wine, chilled

In a blender, combine 1 cup (240 ml) of the water and the guavas and blend to a smooth pulp. Do not blend too long or the seeds will give the pulp a gritty texture.

Strain the mixture through a fine-mesh sieve into a bowl. If the sieve clogs, stir the pulp with a wooden spoon. Slowly add the remaining 1 cup (235 ml) water to the sieve and continue to strain. Discard the seeds and pulp. Add the agave nectar to the bowl and stir. Cover and refrigerate until well chilled, about 1 hour.

Divide the guava mixture evenly among 6 Champagne flutes and top off with the cava. Serve immediately.

 COOK'S NOTE: If you cannot find fresh guavas, use 1¾ cups (425 ml) store-bought guava nectar.

Tissue-Paper Flowers

These tissue-paper flowers are colorful and surprisingly simple to make. I remember in elementary school making a bouquet of them with green pipe cleaners as stems for Mother's Day. This craft is not only easy but also inexpensive, plus the flowers can be used in many different ways: hung on a wall for Mother's Day, as napkin rings for Cinco de Mayo, as part of the centerpiece for the Easter table, or displayed on an altar for Día de los Muertos. They also make wonderful decorations for birthday parties, baby showers, bridal showers, and weddings. You can make the flowers in all shapes, sizes, and colors, customizing them for whatever fiesta is on the calendar.

These tissue-paper flowers go together quickly, but if you are pressed for time, you can buy them premade on Etsy.com.

Materials

Tissue paper, in color or colors of choice

Scissors

Stapler, floral wire, or pipe cleaners

For a large flower, neatly stack 12 sheets of 13 x 20-inch (33 x 50-cm) tissue paper on a work surface. If making smaller flowers, cut the paper into a narrow width and reduce the number of layers. For example, if using tissue paper 8 inches (20 cm) wide, stack only 6 sheets, or if using tissue paper 6 inches wide, stack only 5 sheets.

Starting at a short end, fold the stack accordion-style, making each fold 1 inch (2.5 cm) wide and creasing it well, until you reach the far end. You will end up with a stack 1 inch wide and 13 inches (33 cm) long.

Secure the center of the stack with a stapler, making sure the staple goes through all of the layers. You can also use a length of floral wire or a pipe cleaner, folding it in half, slipping it over the center of the stack, and then twisting it tightly to secure it in place. If using wire, trim the ends as needed.

Using scissors, shape both ends of the stack, rounding them to create more realistic petals.

Now, carefully separate the petal layers. Then, working with one layer at a time, pull from the inside of the layer toward the center of the flower. Spreading each layer from the inside will help keep the paper from tearing. Finally, fluff and shape the flower.

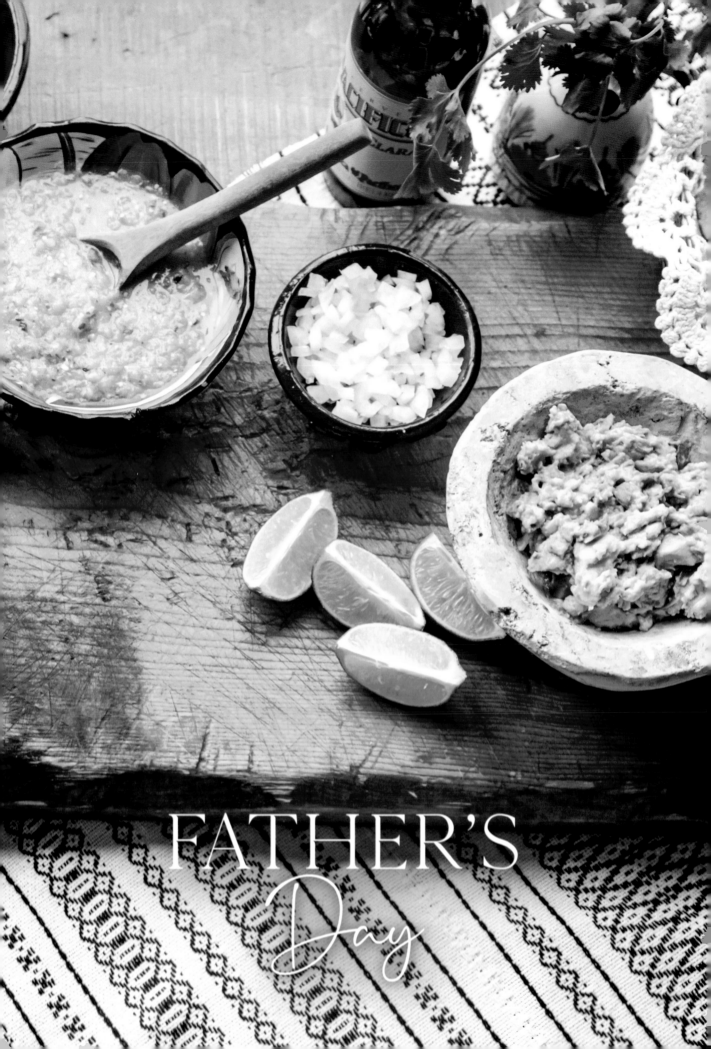

FATHER'S
Day

My children love their daddy, and I am blessed to have such an amazing husband. While we all do a pretty good job of regularly saying "I love you" to one another, taking the opportunity to celebrate him and what he means to our family is an honor we look forward to each June.

When it comes down to it, my husband, Bill, is pretty darn amazing. He's a provider and a protector, my teammate and my soulmate. He's the first person I call with news—good or bad—and my absolute favorite person to snuggle with on the couch. And it has been such a pleasure watching Bill be the best dad and coach to our kids.

If you are lucky enough to have someone (or maybe even several people!) in your life who fills the many roles of a father, then I encourage you to take the time to tell him and show him just how much he means to you.

In our family, we have found that the best gift we can give Dad on Father's Day is a full stomach. Sure, we could take him to a fancy restaurant, but food is our love language. You can start the day off right with meaty Machaca con Huevo. But don't stop there. Lunch and dinner are two more opportunities to feed your fella something absolutely delicious.

My guy is a big fan of any kind of meat, and if your partner is too, show him this chapter. Pork lovers should try Gringa al Pastor, sweet and spicy pieces of pork tucked into a flour tortilla along with lots of melted cheese, or a big batch of crispy carnitas, perfect for loading into warm corn tortillas. Beef lovers should turn to savory sopaipillas filled with a delicious stuffing of ground beef and beans. Be sure to mix up chilled *cheladas* or *micheladas* to serve along with the meal. And don't forget to toast your guy on his special day and to tell him, *te amo, mi amor*.

MACHACA
con Huevo

Machaca, a type of dried meat, is particularly associated with miners in the Mexican state of Chihuahua. Before the arrival of refrigeration, it was common in northern Mexico for miners, ranchers, and cowboys to preserve meat by drying, a practice that extended into Arizona, California, Texas, and New Mexico.

Traditional *machaca* is marinated beef or pork that is rubbed with spices, pounded, dried, and then shredded, much like beef jerky. Back in the old days (before my time), my grandma used to season and dry beef for *machaca*, hanging it with nets that protected it from flies or bugs. The dried meat was then rehydrated and made into flautas, tacos, or burritos. My favorite way to eat *machaca* is with scrambled eggs, tomatoes, and onion for a delicious one-pan breakfast or wrapped in a flour tortilla for a breakfast burrito. I make my *machaca* with leftover shredded cooked brisket, but feel free to used dried beef.

MAKES 6 SERVINGS

1 tablespoon olive oil

½ cup (80 g) chopped red onion

2 Roma tomatoes, chopped

1 jalapeño chile, diced or sliced (optional)

2 cups (440 g) shredded cooked brisket (page 58), or 1 cup (90 g) shredded carne seca (dried beef)

8 large eggs

Salt

Salsa of choice and flour tortillas, warmed, for serving

In a large frying pan pan over medium-high heat, warm the oil. Add the onion and cook, stirring occasionally, until translucent, about 2 minutes. Add the tomatoes, jalapeño (if using), and brisket and cook, stirring occasionally, for 2–3 minutes to mix well and blend the flavors.

Meanwhile, in a bowl, whisk the eggs until blended. Reduce the heat to medium, add the eggs to the frying pan, and cook, stirring, until the eggs are just set, 2–3 minutes. Season to taste with salt.

Remove from the heat and serve at once with the salsa and flour tortillas.

 COOK'S NOTE: Carne seca (dried meat) is available in Latin supermarkets and online.

GRINGA
al Pastor

Dishes described as *al pastor*, literally "shepherd style," originated in Puebla likely as a result of the adoption of the spit-grilled meat introduced by Lebanese immigrants, who began arriving in the late nineteenth century. Similar to Turkish kebab, Greek gyros, and Levantine shawarma, *al pastor* is a prime example of fusion food: a cross between the spit-grilled meat of the Middle East and the guajillo-rubbed grilled pork prepared by Mexican street vendors. A *trompo* (vertical spit) spins slowly on its axis, and most of the *taqueros* place a pineapple on the very top. Traditional *tacos al pastor* are made by warming a small corn tortilla right below the dropping meat being carved from the spit.

This *al pastor* recipe is an easy version that can be made at home whenever the craving hits—no spit or achiote paste needed. That craving hits my daughter often, as this is her absolute favorite dish. She loves anything and everything *al pastor*, especially served on *sopes* (fried corn flour shells) and in tacos.

On a visit to Mexico City, I discovered a number of new dishes, including *tacos arabes* and *gringas al pastor*. *Tacos arabes* are basically Mexican gyro sandwiches wrapped in *pan arabe*, a bread resembling pita but thinner. For *gringas*, meat and cheese are sandwiched between *pan arabe* or thick flour tortillas and then cooked in a hot pan or griddle, and the key here is creamy, melty shredded cheese. A *gringa* is a "foreign woman," and this "sandwich" gets its name because flour tortillas and cheese are popular in the United States. My version of these cheesy, creamy, meaty quesadillas comes with a pineapple salsa—delicious!

— ❦ • ❧ —

MAKE 6 SERVINGS

2 guajillo or New Mexico chiles, stemmed and seeded

3 chipotle chiles in adobo sauce, plus 2 tablespoons of the adobo sauce

4 tablespoons (60 ml) olive oil

Juice of 2 oranges

Continues on the following page

In a bowl, combine the guajillos with hot water to cover and let stand until softened, about 15 minutes. Drain well.

In a blender, combine the softened guajillos, chipotle chiles and adobo sauce, 3 tablespoons of the oil, the orange juice, onion, 4 of the pineapple rings (reserve the remaining rings for the salsa and for grilling), the garlic, salt, and oregano and blend until smooth. Measure 1½ cups (350 ml) of the mixture to use as a marinade. Transfer the remainder to a small bowl, cover, and set aside to serve as a chipotle salsa.

Continued from the previous page

½ red onion, roughly chopped

1 pineapple, peeled, cored, and cut crosswise into rings ¼ inch (6 mm) thick

3 cloves garlic, roughly chopped

2 teaspoons kosher salt

1 teaspoon dried Mexican oregano

2½ lb (1.1 kg) boneless pork loin chops (about 8 chops)

PINEAPPLE SALSA

2–3 pineapple rings, chopped

1 jalapeño chile, diced

¼ cup diced red onion

2 tablespoons fresh lime juice

¼ cup (30 g) chopped fresh cilantro (optional)

Salt

Put the pork chops into a 1-gallon (3.8-l) resealable plastic bag and pour in the marinade. Seal closed, forcing out the air, then massage the pork to distribute the marinade evenly. (Alternatively, put the chops into a shallow dish, pour in the marinade, turn to coat evenly, and cover tightly.) Refrigerate for at least 1 hour, though it is best to leave them overnight to lock in the flavors. Bring to room temperature before grilling.

Meanwhile, make the pineapple salsa. In a bowl, combine the chopped pineapple, jalapeño, onion, lime juice, and cilantro (if using) and mix well. Season with salt, cover, and refrigerate until serving.

Prepare a charcoal or gas grill for direct grilling over medium heat, or preheat a stove-top griddle over medium-high heat.

Remove the pork from the marinade, allowing the excess to drip off. Reserve the marinade. Place the pork on the grill or griddle, working in batches if needed to avoid crowding. Cook until richly browned on the underside, usually 3–4 minutes, then flip and cook until nicely browned on the second side and just cooked through, 3–4 minutes longer. Transfer the pork to a cutting board and let rest for a few minutes, then chop into ¼–½-inch (6–12-mm) pieces and scoop into a large frying pan.

Meanwhile, lightly brush both sides of the remaining pineapple rings with the remaining 1 tablespoon oil. Place on the grill or griddle and cook, turning once, until lightly charred on both sides, about 3 minutes on each side. Transfer to the cutting board, chop into ½-inch (12-mm) pieces, and add to the pork.

Add the reserved marinade to the pan with the pork and pineapple, place over low heat, and heat, stirring occasionally, until the marinade comes to a simmer.

12 flour tortillas, 8 inches
(20 cm) in diameter

Olive oil, for brushing

½ lb (225 g) Oaxaca,
mozzarella, or Muenster
cheese, shredded (about
2 cups)

Chopped fresh cilantro, for
serving

Chopped white onion, for
serving

Lime wedges

Avocado slices, for garnish

To assemble, preheat a large nonstick frying pan over medium-low heat. Lightly brush a tortilla on one side with oil and place, oiled side down, in the hot pan. Top with a generous amount of cheese, followed by the pork-pineapple mixture and then more cheese. Top with a second tortilla and brush the top of the tortilla with oil. Then cover the pan (this helps melt the cheese faster) and cook until the bottom is crisp and golden, 2–3 minutes. Flip and cook until second side is crisp and golden, 1–2 minutes longer. Remove from the pan and keep warm. Repeat with the remaining tortillas, cheese, and pork and pineapple.

Put the cilantro, onion, and lime wedges in small bowls and set out on the table along with the pineapple salsa and remaining chipotle salsa for guests to add to their gringas as desired. Garnish the top of each gringa with avocado slices and serve at once.

SOPAIPILLAS
Stuffed with Beef & Beans

When my hubby and I go out to eat dinner at a Mexican restaurant, he usually orders smothered beef-and-bean-stuffed sopaipillas, a dish popular in New Mexico and Colorado. It is not something I regularly make at home because I don't often cook fried foods. But it is a special-occasion dish and is a perfect choice when you want to treat that special dad in your life on Father's Day.

MAKES ABOUT 8 STUFFED SOPAIPILLAS; 8 SERVINGS

SOPAIPILLAS

2 cups (250 g) all-purpose flour, plus more for dusting

2 teaspoons baking powder

1 teaspoon salt

2 tablespoons solid vegetable shortening

⅔–¾ cup (160–180 ml) lukewarm water

Canola oil, for deep-frying

BEEF AND BEANS

1 tablespoon olive oil

½ cup (80 g) chopped white onion

2 lb (1 kg) lean ground beef

3 cups (500 g) drained Frijoles de la Olla (page 24) or canned pinto beans

2 teaspoons garlic salt

1½ teaspoons ground black pepper

Salt

Continues on the following page

To make the sopaipillas, in a large bowl, whisk together the flour, baking powder, and salt. Add the shortening and, using a pastry blender or your fingers, work the shortening into the flour mixture until the mixture resembles coarse crumbs. Gradually add the water, stirring and tossing with your hands and adding just enough for the dough to pull together. Bring the dough together with your hands, transfer to a lightly floured work surface, and knead the dough until it is smooth, soft, and elastic, 3–5 minutes. Shape into a ball, return the dough to the bowl, cover the bowl with a kitchen towel, and let the dough rest for 15–20 minutes.

Line a sheet pan with parchment paper. Divide the dough in half. On a lightly flour work surface, roll out half of the dough into a round about ⅛ inch (3 mm) thick. Cut the dough into 4-inch (10-cm) squares and transfer them to the prepared sheet pan. Repeat with the remaining dough and add to the pan. Gather up any dough scraps, press together, roll out, and cut out more squares.

To fry the sopaipillas, preheat the oven to 200°F (95°C). Line a second large sheet pan with paper towels and set it near the stove. Pour the oil to a depth of 2 inches (5 cm) into a deep frying pan and heat to 375°F (190°C) on a deep-frying thermometer. When the oil is ready, add 1 square to the pan. It will immediately sink to the bottom and then begin to rise. Fry the square, tapping it a couple of times with a spoon to ensure the dough puffs and creates a pocket. Or, using a spoon, lightly splash a little hot oil on top to ensure it puffs. When the sopaipilla is lightly golden brown on the bottom, flip it over and continue to fry until lightly golden on the second side. The whole frying process should take about 2 minutes. Using a slotted spoon, transfer the sopaipilla to the towel-lined sheet pan and immediately place in the oven to keep warm. Repeat with the remaining squares until all are fried. They can be kept warm in the oven for up to 1 hour before serving.

Continued from the previous page

Shredded Longhorn Colby cheese or chese of your choice, chopped tomato, and shredded iceberg lettuce, for topping

Red Chile Sauce (page 17) or Salsa de Molcajete (page 165), warmed (optional)

COOK'S NOTES: Unstuffed sopaipillas can be cooled and refrigerated in an airtight container for up to 3 days. Reheat in a preheated 350°F (180°C) oven for 10–15 minutes before stuffing and serving.

If you want to add a spice to the stuffing, top the beef-and-bean stuffing with a little warm Red Chile Sauce (page 17) or Salsa de Molcajete (page 165) or with chopped roasted green chiles before topping with cheese, tomato, and lettuce.

Sopaipillas are also a popular dessert, which is what I grew up eating. My grandma served them drizzled with honey.

To prepare the beef and beans, in a large frying pan over medium heat, warm the oil. Add the onion and cook, stirring occasionally, until translucent, about 2 minutes. Add the beef and continue to cook, breaking up the meat and stirring often, until browned, about 5 minutes. Using a potato masher, gently mash the meat so no large chunks remain. Drain off any excess oil from the pan, then return the pan to low heat. Add the beans, garlic salt, and pepper and cook, stirring occasionally and lightly mashing the beans with the meat, until the mixture is heated through and the flavors are blended, about 15 minutes. Season to taste with salt and remove the pan from the heat.

To stuff each warm sopaipilla, slit it in half horizontally and lift off the top. Spoon the warm beef-and-bean mixture onto the bottom. Top with the cheese, tomato, and lettuce and then lightly close the sopaipilla. Serve at once.

If you like smothered sopaipillas, preheat the broiler. Close the sopaipillas after filling with the beef-and-bean mixture, arrange them on a sheet pan, spoon warm chile sauce over the top, sprinkle with the shredded cheese, and broil until the cheese melts, 1–2 minutes. Top with the tomato and lettuce and serve at once.

GRILLED PINEAPPLE
Smoked Mezcal

There are a number of smoke machines and smoke guns on the market that make smoking an individual liquor or a cocktail easy. This drink is basically a pineapple margarita made with grilled pineapple, pineapple juice, lime juice, and mezcal. Mezcal has a smoky flavor because it's made from agave that's cooked with a wood fire in a stone-lined pit. But I add to that natural smokiness with a billowing cool cloud of smoke from a smoke machine. The grilled pineapple adds a rich layer of fruitiness and yet another layer of smoke. If you don't have a cool smoking machine, don't worry. The flavors of this cocktail are outstanding without the addition of smoke.

MAKES 1 COCKTAIL

1 fresh pineapple ring, about 1 inch (2.5) thick, plus 1 fresh pineapple wedge for garnish

1 fl oz (30 ml) fresh lime juice

1 fl oz (30 ml) pineapple juice

¾ fl oz (20 ml) agave nectar or syrup

2 fl oz (60 ml) mezcal or tequila añejo

Ice cubes, plus 1 large cube

Pineapple leaves, for garnish

Preheat a stove-top grill pan over medium-high heat. Add the pineapple ring and wedge and grill, turning once, until seared on both sides, 1–2 minutes. Remove from the grill pan and let cool.

In a cocktail shaker, combine the grilled pineapple ring, lime juice, pineapple juice, and agave nectar and, using a muddler or wooden spoon, muddle them to break down the pineapple ring, releasing its juices. Add the mezcal and fill the shaker two-thirds full with ice. Cover and shake vigorously until the outside of the shaker is lightly frosted.

Put the large ice cube into a rocks glass and strain the cocktail into the glass. If using a smoke machine or gun, smoke the cocktail for 30 seconds. Garnish with the grilled pineapple wedge and pineapple leaves and serve.

CRISPY PORK
Carnitas

Do you like carnitas tender or crispy? This recipe offers you both possibilities.
I have seen carnitas cooked with Coca-Cola or with sweetened condensed milk
for a hint of sweetness. I have added brown sugar, which gives them a touch
of molasses flavor and also adds a lightly caramelized coating. Here I am serving the
carnitas in warm corn tortillas with a squeeze of lime, but they are also wonderful
served atop tostadas or as a filling for burritos, quesadillas, or *tortas*.

MAKES 10–12 SERVINGS

2 tablespoons lard or solid vegetable shortening

3½ lb (1.6 kg) boneless pork shoulder, cut into 5-inch (13-cm) chunks (do not remove fat)

Kosher salt

1½ cups (350 ml) water

Juice of 1 orange

½ white onion, roughly chopped

8 cloves garlic, roughly chopped

2 chipotle peppers in adobo sauce

1 teaspoon dried Mexican oregano

⅛ teaspoon ground cumin

⅛ teaspoon ground cinnamon

1 teaspoon ground black pepper

2 tablespoons packed dark brown sugar

2 fresh thyme sprigs

2 bay leaves

12–16 corn tortillas, warmed, for serving

Roasted Tomatillo Salsa (page 17) and lime wedges, for serving

In a large, deep frying pan or a stockpot over medium-high heat, melt the lard. While the lard is heating, season the pork on all sides with 1 teaspoon salt. When the lard is hot, working in batches to avoid crowding, add the pork and cook, turning once, until browned on both sides, 3–4 minutes on each side. Transfer to a plate and repeat until all the pork is browned.

While the pork is browning, make the braising liquid. In a blender, combine the water, orange juice, onion, garlic, chiles, oregano, cumin, cinnamon, 1 tablespoon salt, and the pepper and blend until smooth.

When all the pork is browned, return it to the pan and pour in the braising liquid. Sprinkle the sugar evenly over the meat and set the thyme sprigs and bay leaves on top. Reduce the heat to medium-low, cover, and cook until the pork is fork-tender, about 1 hour.

If you like carnitas tender, shred the pork or chop it into bite-size pieces and keep warm. If you like carnitas dark and crispy on the outside, heat a large cast-iron frying pan over medium-high heat. Add the pork pieces and cook, turning occasionally, until the liquid has evaporated and the exterior is crispy and caramelized. The timing will depend on how much liquid the pork gave off and how crackly you want the outside. Transfer to a cutting board and chop into bite-size pieces.

Spoon the carnitas onto the warm tortillas and serve with the salsa and lime wedges.

 COOK'S NOTE: For extra crunch and flavor, dress up the carnitas with radish slices and chopped white onion.

MICHELADA & CHELADA

His and hers. I prefer a Mexican lager and my husband prefers a Mexican amber beer. Whatever beer you prefer, it's time for a beer cocktail! Popular throughout Mexico, the *michelada* calls for beer, tomato juice, lime, and hot sauce. It is tangy, spicy, and refreshing and is a great way to elevate a Mexican beer. A *chelada* is much simpler: Mexican beer and fresh lime juice over ice in a salt-rimmed glass.

Michelada with Clamato

MAKES 1 COCKTAIL

Tajín (see Cook's Note, page 78) and a lime wedge, for coating the glass rim

Ice cubes

Juice of 1 lime

½ cup (4 fl oz/ 120 ml) Clamato (clam tomato juice)

1–2 dashes Tabasco sauce

1 bottle or can (12 fl oz/ 350 ml) Mexican lager or amber beer

Celery rib, for garnish (optional)

Pour a little Tajín onto a small, flat plate. Run the lime wedge around the rim of a tall glass, then roll the outer rim in the Tajín, coating it evenly. Fill the glass with ice.

Add the lime juice, Clamato, Tabasco, and beer to the glass and give everything a good stir. Garnish with the celery rib, if using. Enjoy before the ice melts.

Chelada

MAKES 1 COCKTAIL

Coarse salt and a lime wedge, for coating the glass rim

Ice cubes

1 bottle or can (12 fl oz/ 350 ml) Mexican lager or amber beer

2 fl oz (60 ml) fresh lime juice

Pour a little salt onto a small, flat plate. Run the lime wedge around the rim of a tall glass, then roll the outer rim in the salt, coating it evenly. Fill the glass with ice.

Add the lime juice and beer to the glass and stir. Enjoy before the ice melts.

FOURTH OF
July

The Fourth of July has always been one of my favorite holidays. What could be better than a day of food, family, and fireworks? When I was a kid, our family would have huge cookouts at the park or in the backyard of my *tía* Ernestina or my *nina* Valentina. We never went to see a professional fireworks display because my cousins and I would put on our own show.

We'd shoot off bottle rockets, pop off black cats, light up stinky little black snakes, and decorate the sky with sparklers spelling out our names. We would entertain ourselves this way for hours (with no adult supervision, mind you), and thankfully, nobody ever got hurt. But times have changed! Although kid-generated pyrotechnics are no longer part of the day's activities (thank goodness!), what hasn't changed is our dedication to making a special spread of summery foods to share with friends and family. And as proud Mexican Americans, we can really throw down for a backyard barbecue.

To celebrate, we love to put fun, spicy twists on classic American favorites. You like beer brats? I'd bet you'll like them even better with onions, bell peppers, and roasted green chiles. More of a burger lover? Try my Ranchero Burgers with bacon and jalapeños. Pep up either the brats or the burgers with some Chiles en Escabeche for a little extra heat.

Of course, no Fourth of July feast is complete without some tasty sides. Spicy Hatch Chile Potato Salad and Mexican-style street corn are impossible to resist. Dips like Salsa de Molcajete and Mexican Beer Queso Dip are perfect for nibbling with chips as the night goes on.

And that's not all! Steak Fajitas may not be part of your regular cookout menu, but I can guarantee they'll get lots of love from your neighbors. And if any family members or friends don't like to eat red meat, you can always swap in chicken.

To wash it all down, make a big batch of Sandía con Agua Mineral. It's sparkly, kid friendly, and an excellent candidate for spiking with some tequila or vodka for the adults.

Salud, mis amigos! Here's to wishing you a beautiful night of fireworks, both in the sky and on the table!

MEXICAN BEER
Queso Dip

You can count on finding a bowl of *chile con queso* at every fiesta I host. My guests know they can quickly serve themselves some to nibble on with tortilla chips while other guests are arriving. Latinos are notorious for arriving late, so this appetizer is a great way to start the party. I grew up eating a Tex-Mex dip made with processed American cheese. Here I use two types of cheese—Chihuahua and Monterey jack—which I slowly melt in *cerveza*—a definite upgrade from that childhood dip.

MAKES 8–10 SERVINGS

2 tablespoons butter

2 jalapeño chiles, diced

½ cup (60 g) diced white onion

1 can (12 fl oz/350 ml) evaporated milk

1 tablespoon cornstarch

1 teaspoon garlic powder

2 cups (225 g) shredded Chihuahua or Oaxaca cheese

2 cups (225 g) shredded Monterey jack cheese

½ cup (120 ml) Mexican lager beer

3 fresh Anaheim chiles, roasted, peeled, seeded, and chopped (page 15)

Tortilla chips, homemade (page 173) or store-bought, for serving

In a large frying pan over medium-low heat, melt the butter. Add the jalapeños and onion and cook, stirring occasionally, until tender, 4–6 minutes.

Meanwhile, in a bowl, stir together the evaporated milk and cornstarch until the cornstarch dissolves.

When the jalapeños and onion are ready, pour in the milk mixture and stir in the garlic powder. Raise the heat to medium and bring to a gentle boil, stirring constantly. Reduce the heat to low and gradually stir in both cheeses, then continue to stir until melted. Stir in the beer and roasted Anaheims and heat through.

Transfer to a serving bowl and serve at once with the chips.

COOK'S NOTE: The dip thickens as it cools. To reheat it, spoon it into a microwave-safe bowl and microwave on high power for 30–60-second intervals, depending on the amount, stirring after each interval.

HATCH CHILE
Potato Salad

This potato salad is the perfect culinary marriage of me and my hubby. He is of German descent, and this red potato salad has a tangy mustard and vinegar dressing that is reminiscent of a traditional German potato salad. But it also has creamy mayo and roasted green chile in honor of my Mexican heritage.

MAKES 4 SERVINGS

Kosher salt and ground black pepper

1 lb (450 g) small red potatoes (about 10 potatoes), quartered

¼ small red onion, thinly sliced

2 fresh Hatch or Anaheim chiles, roasted, peeled, seeded, and chopped (page 15)

2 teaspoons Dijon mustard

2 tablespoons extra-virgin olive oil

1 tablespoon red wine vinegar

2 tablespoons mayonnaise

2 tablespoons sesame seeds

3 green onions, white and tender green parts, chopped

2 tablespoons chopped fresh cilantro (optional)

Bring a pot of salted water to a rolling boil over medium-high heat. Add the potatoes and cook until fork-tender but not falling apart, 15–18 minutes.

While the potatoes are cooking, in a bowl large enough to hold the finished salad, combine the red onion, chiles, mustard, oil, vinegar, mayonnaise, and sesame seeds and mix well to make a dressing. Season with ½ teaspoon each salt and pepper.

When the potatoes are ready, drain well and toss with the dressing, coating evenly. Add the green onions and cilantro (if using), season with salt and pepper, and toss to mix evenly.

Let cool to room temperature and serve right away, or cover and refrigerate until ready to serve.

 COOK'S NOTE: For a milder version, use 1–2 poblano chiles for the Hatch or Anaheim chiles.

BEER BRATS WITH ONIONS,
Peppers & Roasted Green Chile

These German-style link sausages are simmered in beer before browning on the grill and topped with bell pepper, onion, and green chile in crunchy *bolillos*. These brats remind me of Fourth of July parties during my childhood. I can still see my late German uncle Wolfgang standing at the grill drinking a Tecate and grilling. We ate brats only once a year, which made them special for me. This version was inspired after a trip to a chile farm in Pueblo, Colorado. The people at the farm were grilling beer brats, and instead of serving them in a boring hot dog bun, they tucked them into toasted *bolillos* and topped them with a mountain of goodness similar to a fajita mixture but with spicy green chiles. The use of *bolillos* and the addition of roasted chiles made those brats unforgettable.

MAKES 6 SERVINGS

1 large yellow onion, quartered

½ teaspoon kosher salt

6 raw German bratwursts (preferably Weisswurst)

1 bottle (12 fl oz/350 ml) Mexican amber beer

3 tablespoons butter

1 large white onion, sliced

3 bell peppers, preferably a mix of colors, seeded and cut lengthwise into strips

3 fresh Anaheim or Hatch chiles, roasted, peeled, seeded, and cut lengthwise into strips (page 15)

6 bolillos, homemade (page 232) or store-bought, split and toasted

Spicy mustard, for serving

In a 4-quart (3.8-l) stockpot over medium-high heat, combine the yellow onion, salt, bratwursts, beer, and just enough water to cover the brats and and bring to a low boil. Reduce the heat to a simmer and simmer uncovered, turning the brats occasionally, until firm, 30–40 minutes.

While the brats are simmering, in a seperate pan over medium-high heat, melt the butter. Add the white onion and bell peppers and cook, stirring occasionally, until tender, 5–8 minutes. Stir in the chiles and cook until the chiles are well mixed with the onion and peppers and heated through. Remove from the heat and keep warm.

Prepare a fire in a charcoal or gas grill for direct grilling over medium-high heat.

Remove the sausages from the beer broth and place directly over the fire. Grill, turning as needed, until browned on all sides, 2–4 minutes on each side. Return them to the pot with the beer broth to keep warm until ready to serve.

To serve, tuck a brat into each warm, crusty bolillo, top with the onion-chile mixture, and swab with a little mustard. Serve at once.

RANCHERO
Burgers

These tasty burgers are made from a mixture of ground beef and crumbled cooked bacon, Cheddar cheese, and a little jalapeño heat and are served on soft ciabatta or brioche buns—a delicious riff on a classic Fourth of July party dish.

———— ❧•❧ ————

MAKES 5–6 BURGERS, DEPENDING ON SIZE

2 lb (1 kg) lean ground beef, at least 80 percent lean

5 slices bacon, cooked until crisp and crumbled

1 teaspoon salt

1 teaspoon ground black pepper

1 teaspoon onion powder

½ teaspoon garlic powder

1 jalapeño chile, diced

1 cup (115 g) shredded Cheddar cheese

5–6 soft ciabatta or brioche hamburger buns, split

1 avocado, halved, pitted, peeled, and mashed

1 medium red onion, sliced into rings

1 Anaheim or poblano chile, roasted, peeled, seeded, and cut lengthwise into strips (page 15), optional

2 medium tomatoes, sliced

5–6 iceberg or other lettuce leaves

Prepare a charcoal or gas grill for direct grilling over medium heat.

In a large bowl, combine the beef, bacon, salt, pepper, onion powder, garlic powder, jalapeño, and cheese and mix well. Divide the mixture into 5 or 6 equal portions. Shape each portion into a ball, then gently flatten into a patty about ½ inch thick.

Place the patties on the grill and cook, turning once, for 8–10 minutes total for medium to medium-well. During the final 2 minutes, place the bun halves, cut side down, on the grill to toast. Remove the burgers and buns from the grill.

Arrange the bun bottoms, cut side up, on a work surface and spread with the avocado. Top with the lettuce, tomato slices, onion rings, burgers, and chile strips. Close with the bun tops and serve.

COOK'S NOTE: If you don't have a grill or don't feel like setting up the grill, cook the burgers in a lightly oiled cast-iron frying pan on the stove top over medium-high heat.

STEAK *Fajitas*

There is nothing like a sizzling frying pan of fajitas being served to your table. When I think of Tex-Mex comfort foods, delicious beef dinners and steak fajitas are at the top of my list of favorites. Tex-Mex is a beautiful blend of a little bit of Texas, a little bit of Mexico, and a whole lot of flavor! My mom and I always share an order of fajitas when we eat out, and now my daughter, Maya, and I do the same.

———— ❧ • ❧ ————

MAKES 8 SERVINGS

¾ cup (180 ml) fresh lime juice

4 tablespoons (60 ml) vegetable oil

4 cloves garlic, minced

2 tablespoons chili powder

¼ teaspoon ground cumin

¾ teaspoon salt

¼ teaspoon ground black pepper

2 lb (1 kg) flank steak

1 large red bell pepper, seeded and cut lengthwise into strips

1 large yellow bell pepper, seeded and cut lengthwise into strips

12 large green onions, white and tender green parts, sliced into 2-inch (5-cm) pieces on the diagonal

Shredded Longhorn Colby or Cheddar cheese, Mexican crema or sour cream, pico de gallo or other fresh salsa of choice, and/or guacamole (page 102), for topping

16 flour tortillas, about 6 inches (15 cm) in diameter, warmed

In a small bowl, combine the lime juice, 2 tablespoons of the oil, the garlic, chili powder, cumin, salt, and black pepper and mix well to make a marinade. Put the steak into a 1-gallon (3.8-l) resealable plastic bag and pour in the marinade. Seal closed, forcing out the air, then massage the steak and turn the bag to distribute the marinade evenly. (Alternatively, put the steak into a shallow dish, pour in the marinade, turn to coat evenly, and cover tightly.) Marinate in the refrigerator for at least 2 hours or for up to 8 hours, turning the bag once or twice.

Remove the steak from the marinade, place on a cutting board, and thinly slice on the diagonal against the grain. Return the slices to the marinade and set aside while you cook the bell peppers and green onions.

In a large frying pan over medium-high heat, warm 1 tablespoon of the oil. Add the bell peppers and green onions and cook, stirring often, until tender, 3–5 minutes. Transfer to a bowl and keep warm. Put your choice of toppings in individual small bowls and set out on the table.

Drain the steak strips, discarding the marinade. Return the pan to medium-high heat and add the remaining 1 tablespoon oil. When the oil is hot, add the steak and cook, stirring occasionally, until no longer pink, about 3 minutes. Remove from the heat.

Scoop the steak and the peppers and onions into the warm tortillas, fold in half, and serve. Invite guests to add toppings as desired.

 COOK'S NOTE: You can substitute 2 lb (1 kg) boneless, skinless chicken breast for the skirt steak.

CHILES en Escabeche

Also known as *chiles en vinagre* or *chiles curtidos*, these tangy-hot, slightly
sweet pickled chiles are the perfect accompaniment to *tortas* (sandwiches) or anytime you
want a bite of spice.

—— ⟟•⟟ ——

**MAKES FOUR–FIVE ¾-PINT
(350-ML) JARS**

2 cups (475 ml) water

2 cups (475 ml) distilled white
vinegar

1 tablespoon sugar

1 tablespoon kosher salt

1 teaspoon dried Mexican
oregano

1 teaspoon black peppercorns

2 bay leaves

1 clove garlic, smashed

5 large jalapeño chiles, sliced
into rings ⅛ inch (3 mm) wide

2 serrano chiles, sliced into
rings ⅛ inch (3 mm) wide

4 carrots, peeled and cut into
rounds ⅛ inch (3 mm) thick

1 sweet yellow onion, sliced

Have ready four–five ¾-pint (350-ml) jars with tight-fitting lids.
Run them through the dishwasher or wash them in hot, soapy water.
Drain well.

In a small stockpot over high heat, combine the water, vinegar, sugar,
salt, oregano, peppercorns, bay leaves, and garlic and bring to a boil.
Reduce the heat to medium-high and stir in the jalapeños, serranos,
carrots, and onion and cook until the chiles turn from bright green to
a slightly duller green, 10–15 minutes. Remove from the heat.

Remove and discard the garlic clove and the bay leaves. Using a
slotted spoon, transfer the chile mixture to the jars, dividing it evenly
among the jars and trying to get a roughly equal number of chile,
carrot, and onion slices in each jar. Ladle the pickling liquid into the
jars, filling to within ½ inch (12 mm) below the rim.

Cover the jars tightly, then let cool completely and refrigerate for up
to 2 months. Once opened, a jar will keep for up to 1 month.

ELOTE

Whenever I pass a street vendor selling *elote*, I quickly whip a U-turn. I honestly can't resist Mexican-style street corn. The combination of roasted corn smeared with butter and mayo, sprinkled with salty grated queso Cotija and Tajín, and drizzled with a squeeze of fresh lime juice and spicy hot sauce instantly makes my mouth water.

Grill the corn, set out the toppings, and let your guests dress up their ears of corn as they like. Sweet, spicy, salty, and tangy—the mix of toppings is an explosion of Latin flavors that you will crave all summer long. This simple recipe promises to be the smash hit of any Fourth of July barbecue.

MAKES 4 SERVINGS

4 ears corn, with husks intact

2 tablespoons olive oil

FOR TOPPING

Unsalted butter, at room temperature

Mayonnaise

Finely grated Cotija or Parmesan cheese

Salt

Tajín (see Cook's Note, page 78) or ground dried chile

Lime wedges

Valentina or other Mexican hot sauce

Working with 1 corn ear at a time, carefully pull back the husks, leaving them attached at the stem end, then remove the silk and rinse the ear. Pull the husks back up over the corn, covering the ear. Fill a large pot with water and immerse the corn ears in the water for about 20 minutes. This helps prevent the husks from burning on the grill. Just before grilling, remove from the pot and shake off the excess water.

Meanwhile, prepare a charcoal or gas grill for direct heat grilling over medium-high heat.

Lightly brush the corn husks with the oil. Place the corn on the grill and cook, turning the ears about every 3 minutes, until the kernels are tender and slightly charred, 12–15 minutes total. While the corn is grilling, set all the toppings on the table.

Remove the corn from the grill and, protecting your hands against the heat, pull off (or pull back and tie) the husks. Invite your guests to garnish their corn as they like. The traditional way to dress up grilled corn is to spread on a layer of butter, followed by a layer of mayonnaise. Next, sprinkle with crumbled cheese and then finish with a sprinkle of salt, a little Tajín, a squeeze of lime juice, and a drizzle of hot sauce.

 COOK'S NOTE: If you are not a fan of mayonnaise, substitute Mexican crema or sour cream for the mayonnaise.

SALSA
de Molcajete

This rich and smoky salsa is easy to make with or without a *molcajete* and *tejolote*, the traditional lava-stone mortar and pestle (see Cook's Notes). The ingredients are readily available, and if you like your food extra spicy, be sure to add the árbol chiles to the mix. All the ingredients are roasted on a hot *comal* (cast-iron griddle) before they are ground together in the *molcajete*. This salsa is also known as *salsa tatemada* or fire-roasted salsa.

MAKES ABOUT 2 CUPS (475 ML)

6 Roma tomatoes, halved

3 jalapeño or serrano chiles, stemmed

2 dried árbol chiles, stemmed (optional)

2 cloves garlic, unpeeled

1 teaspoon salt

Preheat a comal or cast-iron frying pan over medium-high heat. Place the tomatoes, jalapeño chiles, árbol chiles (if using), and garlic on the hot pan. Roast, turning as needed, until lightly charred. The garlic and árbol chiles (if using) will be ready first; remove them after 2–3 minutes to prevent burning. Continue roasting the remaining ingredients until charred on all sides, 8–10 minutes. Remove from the pan.

Peel the garlic cloves. Do not peel the fresh chiles or the tomatoes. Drop the garlic cloves into the molcajete, add the salt, and, using the tejolote, grind together the garlic and salt until a paste forms. Add the árbol chiles, if using, and grind until well incorporated with the garlic-salt paste. Now add the roasted jalapeños, one at a time, grinding after each addition until incorporated. Then add the roasted tomatoes, a half at a time, and mash until well mixed but the salsa is still chunky. Taste and adjust the seasoning with salt if needed.

Serve immediately, or store in an airtight container in the refrigerator for up to1 week.

 COOK'S NOTES: Substitute 1 can (15 oz/425 g) fire-roasted tomatoes for the fresh tomatoes.

If you don't have a molcajete, mash the ingredients with a bean masher or pulse the ingredients in a food processor or blender.

To simplify cleanup of the comal or frying pan, line it with aluminum foil.

SANDIA
con Agua Mineral

You might have seen *vitroleros* (barrel-shaped glass jars) filled with colorful *aguas frescas* in Mexican markets, which is the typical way these vibrant, refreshing drinks are displayed for sale. They come in a variety of flavors, with *agua de sandía* (watermelon water) especially popular in the summer when watermelons are abundant. If you like a traditional *agua fresca*, use tap water instead of bubbly mineral water. I am obsessed with Topo Chico (see headnote, page 293), and the combination of watermelon and this mineral water delivers a wonderful mix of flavor, balance, and sparkle.

MAKES 2 QUARTS (1.9 L)

8 cups (1.2 kg) cubed seedless watermelon

1 cup (240 ml) simple syrup (see Cook's Notes)

¼ cup (60 ml) fresh lime juice

4 cups (950 ml) mineral water (preferably Topo Chico), chilled

Lime slices, for garnish (optional)

Small fresh mint sprigs, for garnish (optional)

In a blender, combine half each of the watermelon and simple syrup and purée until smooth. Pour through a coarse-mesh sieve into a large pitcher. Repeat with the remaining watermelon and simple syrup and add to the pitcher. Stir in the lime juice, then cover and refrigerate until well chilled.

Just before serving, pour in the mineral water and stir well. Serve in tall glasses and garnish with the lime slices and mint if desired.

COOK'S NOTES: To make a simple syrup, in a saucepan over medium heat, combine 1 cup (240 ml) water and 1 cup (200 g) sugar and bring to a simmer, stirring until the sugar dissolves. Remove from the heat and let cool before using.

Leftover watermelon sparkling water will keep in the refrigerator for up to 3 days. Or you can freeze it in ice-pop molds for a super-refreshing summer treat.

Un vaso de agua
no se le niega a nadie

MEXICAN *Independence Day*

On September 16, 1810, priest and community leader Father Hidalgo made what is now known as El Grito de Dolores (The Cry of Dolores), urging his fellow citizens to fight for their independence from Spain after nearly three hundred years of colonial rule. To this day, Mexicans around the world celebrate the anniversary of his call as our day of independence.

Many people in the United States commonly mistake Cinco de Mayo (see page 92) for Mexican Independence Day. But while Cinco de Mayo celebrates a single victory in 1862 over the French in the ongoing Franco-Mexican War—a war that Mexico eventually lost—September 16 represents the beginning of an historic eleven-year war against Spain that ended with Mexico's independence.

In the United States, Mexican Independence Day, which kicks off National Hispanic Heritage Month, is celebrated in much the same way as the Fourth of July—with fireworks, music, dancing, family get-togethers, and, of course, lots of delicious food and drink.

Sweet and tangy Agua de Tamarindo is the perfect Mexican beverage for the day. It's deeply refreshing, nonalcoholic, and ideal for cleansing the palate for my Tequila Tasting Party. It also happens to make a mean cocktail (page 198)! As for food, creamy Chiles en Nogada, a specialty of Puebla, and Flautas de Carne Deshebrada a la Bandera, which are topped with green salsa, Mexican *crema*, and tomato broth—the colors of the Mexican flag—are two delicious celebratory dishes everyone will enjoy.

Regardless of whether or not you share any Hispanic heritage, I hope you will take this opportunity to send summer off in style. After all, we can all use more fiestas! From my family to yours, *Feliz Día de la Independencia, y Viva México!*

Chiquitita
pero picosa

LIME CORN
Tortilla Chips

You just can't beat homemade corn tortilla chips. They are so easy to make and so addicting. These are flavored with lime and scream *ajúa!*

MAKES 48 CHIPS

12 corn tortillas, quartered

¼ cup (60 ml) fresh lime juice

Canola or peanut oil, for frying

2 teaspoons coarse salt

Grated zest of 2 limes

Set enough wire racks on sheet pans to hold all the tortilla quarters in a single layer. One at a time, brush each tortilla quarter on both sides with lime juice and place on a rack. Let dry until there are no visible signs of moisture on the quarters, at least 1 hour.

Line a sheet pan with paper towels and set it near the stove. Pour the oil to a depth of 1 inch (2.5 cm) into a large, deep frying pan and heat over medium-high heat to 350°F (180°C) on a deep-frying thermometer, or until a small piece of tortilla dropped into the oil sizzles on contact.

Working in batches to avoid crowding the pan, carefully drop a handful of the tortilla quarters into the hot oil and fry until they turn a beautiful golden yellow, 2–3 minutes. Using tongs or a slotted spoon, transfer to the towel-lined sheet pan to drain. Season immediately with some of the salt and lime zest, then fry, drain, and season the remaining tortilla quarters the same way.

Serve the tortilla chips warm or at room temperature. Lightly cover any leftover chips with a paper towel at room temperature for up to 2 days. Do not store in an airtight container or they will become soggy and stale.

FLAUTAS
de Carne Deshebrada a la Bandera

These panfried crispy tacos, known as flautas or *tacos dorados*, are filled with tender shredded beef brisket just like my grandma used to make. They are topped with an avocado and tomatillo salsa, Mexican *crema*, and tomato broth, the colors of the Mexican flag (*bandera*), making the finished dish the ideal centerpiece for a festive Mexican Independence Day feast. For a spicy option, serve with red chile sauce instead of mild tomato broth.

— ✧ • ✧ —

MAKES 8–10 SERVINGS

BEEF BRISKET

1 beef brisket or boneless beef chuck roast, 2–2½ lb (1–1.1 kg), trimmed of fat

3 bay leaves

3 cloves garlic, peeled

½ teaspoon peppercorn medley

½ teaspoon black peppercorns

1 tablespoon salt

1 teaspoon ground black pepper

2 cups (475 ml) water

AVOCADO-TOMATILLO SALSA

4 tomatillos, husked and rinsed

2 jalapeño chiles, stemmed

1 clove garlic, unpeeled

3 avocados, halved, pitted, and peeled

Handful of fresh cilantro sprigs

1 teaspoon salt

Continues on the following page

To make the brisket, preheat a large, deep frying pan over medium heat. Add the brisket and sear, turning once, until a nice brown crust forms on both sides, about 5 minutes on each side.

Transfer the brisket to a plate or cutting board. Make 3 evenly spaced slits, each 3 inches (7.5 cm) deep, in the meat. Insert 1 of the bay leaves, 1 of the garlic cloves, and one-third of the peppercorns into each slit. Place the brisket, salt, ground pepper, and water in a slow cooker. Cover and cook on the low setting until fork-tender, about 6 hours, turning the brisket after 3 hours.

While the brisket is cooking, make the salsa. Preheat the broiler. Line a sheet pan with aluminum foil and arrange the tomatillos, jalapeños, and garlic on the pan. Place under the broiler and broil until blackened on top, about 5 minutes, then flip everything over and broil until blackened on the second side, 4–5 minutes. Watch the tomatillos to make sure they are not burning.

Remove the pan from the broiler. Slip the jalapeños into a small plastic bag, close the top, and let steam until the skins loosen, about 10 minutes. Meanwhile, peel the garlic and let the tomatillos cool. When the jalapeños are ready, remove from the bag and peel away the blackened skin.

In a blender, combine the tomatillos, jalapeños, garlic, avocados, cilantro, and salt and blend until smooth and creamy, adding water as needed to achieve a good consistency. Transfer to a bowl, cover, and set aside.

Continued from the previous page

1 can (28 oz/875 g) whole tomatoes

¼ white onion, roughly chopped

2 cloves garlic, roughly chopped

½ teaspoon dried Mexican oregano

¼ teaspoon salt

¼ teaspoon ground black pepper

¼ cup (60 ml) water

24–30 corn tortillas

Canola oil, for deep-frying

2 cups (475 ml) Mexican crema

COOK'S NOTES: To save time, use store-bought red salsa and green salsa in place of the tomato broth and avocado-tomatillo salsa.

Make a slurry of equal parts all-purpose flour and water and use in place of the toothpicks, brushing it along the edge of the tortilla and then pressing to seal.

To make the tomato broth, rinse out the blender, then add the tomatoes and their juices, onion, garlic, oregano, salt, pepper, and water and purée until smooth. Just before serving, pour the mixture into a saucepan, bring to a boil over medium-high heat, reduce the heat to low, and keep warm until serving.

When the brisket is ready, transfer it to a cutting board, discard the bay leaves and peppercorns, and let rest for a few minutes to firm up. Coarsely shred the meat, then cut it into small bite-size pieces. Return the meat to the slow cooker and allow it to soak up all the cooking juices.

Heat a comal (cast-iron griddle) or heavy frying pan over low heat. To assemble each flauta, warm a tortilla on the comal, turning it once, until pliable, about 20 seconds on each side. Spoon a little shredded brisket down the center of the tortilla (you need only about 2 tablespoons), then roll up the tortilla tightly around the filling and secure the roll with a toothpick. Be sure the roll is tight so the filling does not escape during frying. Repeat to make more flautas until all the brisket is used.

Preheat the oven to 200°F (95°C). Line a sheet pan with paper towels and set it near the stove. Pour the oil to a depth of 2 inches (5 cm) into a deep, heavy pot and heat over medium heat to 375°F (190°C) on a deep-frying thermometer. Working in batches to avoid crowding the pan, carefully slide the flautas into the hot oil. Fry, using tongs to turn them over at least once, until crispy and lightly golden, 2–3 minutes. Using the tongs, transfer to the towel-lined sheet pan to drain and place in the oven to keep warm. Repeat until all the flautas are fried.

Remove the toothpicks and serve the flautas piping hot topped with stripes of the salsa, crema, and tomato broth to simulate the flag of Mexico.

CHILES *en Nogada*

I was first introduced to *chiles en nogada* when I saw the movie *Like Water for Chocolate*. The film is about love, tradition, passion, communication, and food. At the end, Tita and Chencha are busy preparing the ingredients—roasting chiles, soaking and shelling walnuts, breaking open pomegranates—for this classic dish of roasted poblanos stuffed with a mixture of meat and fruit and topped with a creamy nut sauce.

I did not grow up eating *chiles en nogada*, which originated in Puebla and is enjoyed throughout central Mexico on Independence Day because its colors—green chiles, white sauce, red pomegranate seeds—are the colors of the national flag. Although my grandma was born in Mexico, she never made this recipe. She was from Chihuahua, in northern Mexico, and I'm not sure she ever even encountered this dish.

Traditionally, the sauce is made with freshly shelled walnuts, which are first soaked overnight in milk and skinned to eliminate bitterness. This is a tedious process. Instead, I toast the walnuts and then shake them in a sieve to remove the skins.

MAKES ABOUT 6 SERVINGS

6 poblano chiles

1 tablespoon olive oil

½ white onion, finely chopped

3 cloves garlic, minced

1 lb (450 g) ground pork

½ lb (225 g) ground beef

1½ teaspoons dried Mexican oregano

½ teaspoon salt

½ teaspoon dried thyme

½ teaspoon ground nutmeg

¼ teaspoon ground black pepper

⅛ teaspoon ground cloves

⅛ teaspoon ground cinnamon

1 Roma tomato, chopped

Continues on the following page

Preheat the broiler. Line a sheet pan with aluminum foil. Arrange the chiles on the pan and then pierce each chile with the tip of a knife.

Place the pan under the broiler and broil the chiles, watching them closely as the skin will blister and turn black within minutes. After 3–5 minutes, turn the chiles as needed so they blister on all sides. They are ready when the skins are evenly blistered and mostly black.

Remove from the broiler, slip the chiles into a plastic bag, close the top, and let steam until the skins loosen, about 10 minutes. Remove from the bag and peel off the blackened skin. Using a small, sharp knife, carefully slit each chile open from about ½ inch (12 mm) below the stem area to within about ½ inch (12 mm) of the tip and open gently. Carefully remove the seeds, leaving the stems attached. Set the chiles aside to fill later.

In a large frying pan over medium heat, warm the oil. Add the onion and cook, stirring occasionally, until translucent, about 2 minutes. Add the garlic and continue to cook, stirring, for 1 minute. Add the pork, beef, oregano, salt, thyme, nutmeg, pepper, cloves, and cinnamon and cook, stirring and breaking up the meat, until the meat is cooked, about 8 minutes. Add the tomato, apple, pear, wine, and parsley, stir well, and continue to cook, stirring occasionally, for 5 minutes. Then cover and cook until the fruits soften, about 5 minutes longer. Uncover, add the raisins, and continue to cook

Continued from the previous page

1 Gala or Golden Delicious apple, halved, cored, peeled, and chopped

1 Bartlett pear, halved, cored, peeled, and chopped

2 tablespoons white wine

¼ cup (15 g) chopped fresh flat-leaf parsley

½ cup (80 g) raisins

WALNUT SAUCE

1 cup (115 g) walnuts

¼ cup (60 ml) whole milk, plus more if needed

½ cup (120 ml) Mexican crema

2 tablespoons white wine

¼ lb (115 g) cream cheese, at room temperature

2 oz (60 g) fresh goat cheese, at room temperature

2 tablespoons sugar

Pomegranate seeds and chopped fresh flat-leaf parsley, for garnish

uncovered, stirring often, for 10 minutes to blend the flavors. Taste and adjust the seasoning with salt and pepper if needed. Remove from the heat and keep warm until using.

To make the sauce, preheat the oven to 400°F (200°C). Spread the nuts in a single layer on a sheet pan, place in the oven, and toast, shaking the pan once or twice so they toast evenly, until fragrant and the skins are crispy, 8 minutes.

Remove the nuts from the oven, let cool briefly, and then rub them, a few at a time, between two kitchen towels to loosen the skins. Transfer the nuts to a fine-mesh sieve and shake well. The skins will flake off, leaving you with clean nuts.

In a blender, combine the milk, crema, wine, cream cheese, goat cheese, and walnuts and blend until you have a smooth, thick sauce, adding more milk as needed to make the mixture creamy. Add the sugar and blend just until dissolved.

Stuff the filling into the poblanos, packing them until they are plump but will still close. Place the stuffed chiles on individual plates or a large serving plate. Pour the sauce over the chiles, garnish with the pomegranate seeds and parsley, and serve.

 COOK'S NOTE: This recipe is easily doubled for a large group.

STRAWBERRY &
Pistachio Paletas

These tricolor ice pops—green, white, and red—are yet another great addition to your Independence Day menu. You might want to explain to any kids at your celebration the significance of the three background colors of the Mexican flag: green represents hope, white stands for purity, and red symbolizes the color of blood of those who died fighting for independence.

MAKES SIX 3-OZ (90-G) ICE POPS

¼ cup (30 g) pistachios, finely chopped

½ cup (100 g) plain Greek yogurt

1 cup (240 ml) coconut, almond, or rice milk

3 tablespoons agave nectar or honey

2 drops green food coloring (optional)

¼ cup (30 g) pistachios

1 cup (140 g) strawberries, stemmed

2 tablespoons water

In a food processor, pulse the pistachios until finely ground. Set aside.

Have ready 6 ice pop molds. In a bowl, whisk together the yogurt, milk, and agave nectar. Divide the mixture evenly between 2 small bowls.

Add the ground pistachios and the food coloring (if using) to the yogurt mixture in 1 bowl and stir to mix well. Divide the pistachio-yogurt mixture evenly among the ice pop molds and freeze until it begins to set, about 1 hour.

After the hour, insert the sticks into the molds and then top the pistachio layer with the white yogurt layer, dividing it evenly. Return the molds to the freezer and freeze until the white layer begins to set, about 1 hour.

Meanwhile, in the processor or a blender, combine the strawberries and water and purée until smooth.

After the second hour, top the white layer with a strawberry layer, dividing the mixture evenly. Return the molds to the freezer and freeze until solid, about 4 hours, before serving.

To serve, briefly run the molds under lukewarm water to loosen the ice pops. Serve right away.

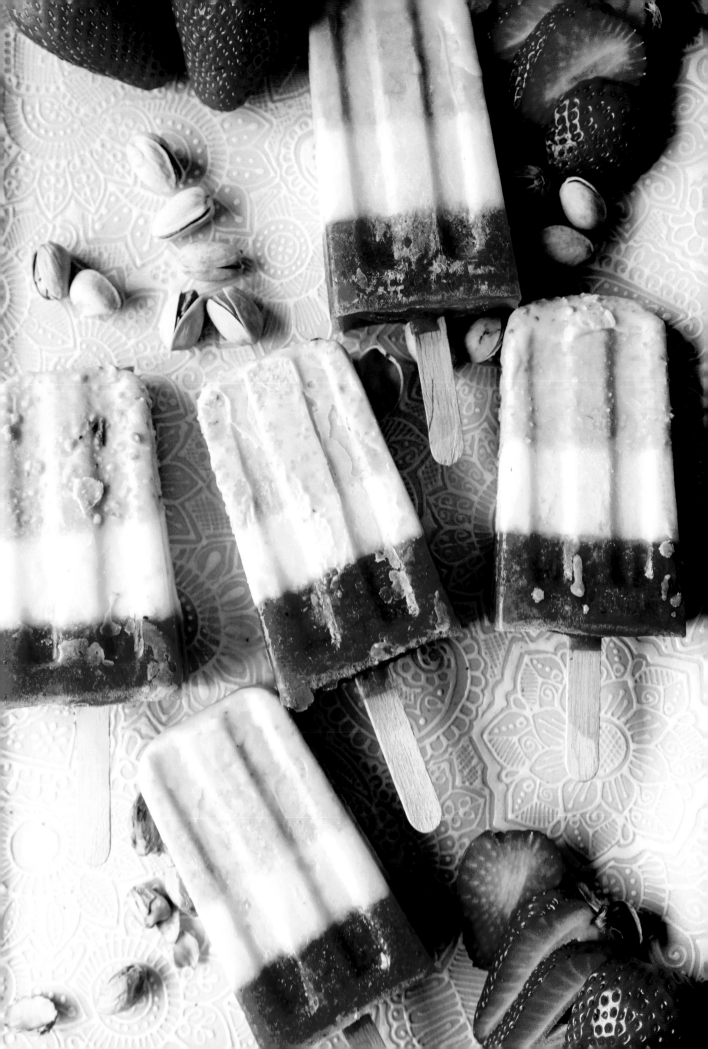

AGUA

de Tamarindo

This *agua fresca*, which looks like a beautiful summer tea, has an exotic sweet and tangy flavor. Tamarind pods can be found in most Latin supermarkets and some Asian markets. If you don't have a source near you, look for the pods online.

MAKES 10–12 SERVINGS

15 tamarind pods

8 cups (1.9 l) water, plus more if needed

¾ cup (150 g) sugar, plus more if needed

Ice cubes, for serving

Remove and discard the hard outer shell from each tamarind pod. Some skins may stick, and that is okay.

In a saucepan over high heat, combine the tamarind and 4 cups (950 ml) of the water, bring to a boil, and boil for 2 minutes. As the tamarind boils, mash it with a potato masher, then remove from the heat, cover, and let steep for about 30 minutes.

Pour the tamarind mixture through a fine-mesh sieve placed over a pitcher, pushing as much liquid through as possible and discarding the pulp, peels, strings, and seeds remaining in the sieve.

Add the sugar and the remaining 4 cups (950 ml) water and stir until the sugar dissolves. Taste and add more sugar and/or water if needed. The agua fresca will keep in a tightly capped container in the refrigerator for up to 1 week.

Pour over ice to serve.

TEQUILA
Tasting Party

As I'm sure you've already guessed, tequila is one of my favorite spirits. It also happens to be a little misunderstood. Many people seem to believe that tequila is just for margaritas, or only remember the cheap, hangover-inducing shots of their youth. Amigos, I'm here to tell you that tequila can be just as highbrow and varied as a fancy bourbon, bottle of wine, or microbrew beer.

To learn more about this widely appreciated spirit, I strongly recommend hosting a tequila tasting party. Not only is a party centered on booze a fun premise, but the education you and your friends are sure to take away from the experience will make the night truly special.

First, a primer on tequila types is needed. There are three primary types of tequila, all of which are made from blue agave and by law must be made in one of five Mexican states.

Blanco   Reposado   Añejo

Blanco

The lightest and youngest of the tequila types, blanco is sometimes sold as "silver" tequila. Blancos are perhaps the truest expression of the flavor characteristics of agave, as they are never aged in wood. They have a bright, citrusy quality that lends itself to mixology.

Reposado

This is the Goldilocks of the tequila bunch. It is aged for two to twelve months in steel or wooden barrels, lending it a golden hue. The aging process leads to both oaky, vanilla flavors and some of the bright tastes for which blanco is revered. Reposado can stand up to many flavors, making it a favorite of bartenders. It is also a great sipping tequila.

Añejo

If you're a fan of aged whiskey, I think you'll enjoy añejo. Aged for at least a year in wooden barrels, this is the darkest and most complex of the tequila types. Heavy notes of honey, vanilla, and spice come through, making it excellent for sipping on the rocks.

To do a proper tasting, I suggest starting with at least one bottle from each of the three primary tequila types.

When it comes time to serve, be sure to go in order of age, starting with the youngest (blanco) and moving toward the more complex, older spirits. I suggest investing in a set of champagne flutes, which are inexpensive, easy to sniff from, and versatile. Depending on the size of your party and your budget, you can opt to rent glasses so everyone has a clean glass each time a new tequila is being tasted.

There is also a proper method of tasting. First, use your nose. Start by sniffing the glass from several inches (10–15 cm) away, then slowly bring the glass closer to your nose. After sniffing, give the tequila a little "kiss"—in other words, small sips. You don't need to be fancy. There's no swirling it around the tongue, for example. Just take a few small sips and really concentrate on the flavors. Ask your guests what flavors they taste. It's not a test but rather just a fun conversation.

If you want to be fancy, after tasting each tequila, have your guests take a deep whiff of coffee beans. Although this isn't necessary, it does help to refresh your palate and prepare your mind to receive the new scents, flavors, and mouthfeel of the next bottle.

In a traditional tequila tasting, nibbles are served after, never during, the educational tasting. That way, guests can focus on the flavors in the glass rather than the tequila competing with food. But since we aren't professionals, have fun! Serve some simple appetizers, such as chips, salsas, guacamole, and other easy finger foods.

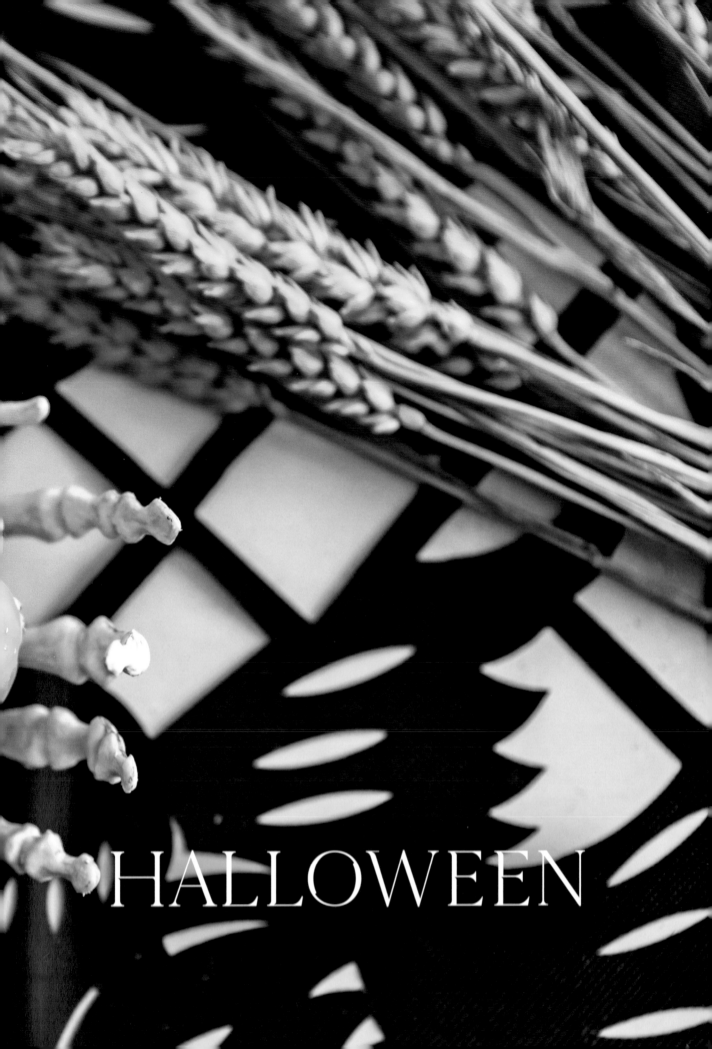

HALLOWEEN

As a deeply creative person, Halloween has always been one of my favorite holidays. I love going over the top with costumes, which I can thank my mom for. When I was little, she used her incredible talents as a seamstress to create jaw-dropping renditions of the characters I wanted to become. She made some beautiful costumes for me that I saved and that my kids have even worn—jester, genie, and witch, among others! While I love continuing this transformative tradition for my own kids, I have to stick to no-sew costumes and love sourcing great finds at thrift stores.

There are plenty of other ways, in addition to costumes, to showcase creativity during this spookiest time of the year. Our family loves to host costume parties, and my kids like to deck out our home for Halloween. Carved pumpkins, spiderwebs, bloody handprints, and our life-size *esqueleto* (skeleton) all make an annual appearance.

While trick-or-treating is always on the agenda, I like to serve a nourishing, cozy meal with all the flavors of fall before heading out. After carving jack-o'-lanterns, pumpkin seeds abound. Instead of tossing them out, turn them into Spicy Roasted Pepitas! They're a tasty and healthy snack that pairs beautifully with my tequila-based El Ojo cocktail or are delicious sprinkled atop Calabaza en Tacha, a dessert of candied pumpkin that is perfect for the season.

Before appetites are ruined on fistfuls of candy, I like to serve a hearty main like Chile Colorado con Carne y Papas. This red chile beef stew is the perfect way to warm up from the inside out. And if you are hosting a Halloween fiesta, try making a platter of boo-tiful Witches' Fingers Sugar Cookies.

No matter how you and your family celebrate, I hope you enjoy autumn's approach as much as we do. These Halloween-inspired recipes are always a perfect way to get us into the *spirit* of the season!

SPICY ROASTED
Pepitas

Plain pumpkin seeds get a kick from ancho chile powder, making them a delightfully crunchy and addictive appetizer for your Halloween celebration.

MAKES ABOUT 1⅔ CUPS (225 G)

½ lb (225 g) raw pepitas (hull-free pumpkin seeds; see Cook's Note)

1 teaspoon ancho chile powder

1 teaspoon ground paprika

½ teaspoon kosher salt

⅛ teaspoon garlic powder

1 tablespoon olive oil

2 teaspoons fresh lime juice

Preheat the oven to 350°F (180°C). Line a large sheet pan with parchment paper.

Put the pepitas into a bowl. Sprinkle with the chile powder, paprika, salt, and garlic powder, drizzle with the oil and lime juice, and toss to coat evenly. Pour the pepitas onto the prepared sheet pan and spread in an even layer.

Roast, stirring once after about 6 minutes, until lightly toasted, about 12 minutes. Let cool before serving. The pepitas will keep in an airtight container at room temperature for up to 1 week.

COOK'S NOTE: If you are using seeds from a fresh pumpkin, scoop them out and separate them from the pulp and fibrous strands. An easy way to do this is to immerse the seeds in a bowl of water; the seeds will float to the top and can be lifted out with a slotted spoon, leaving the pulp and fibers at the bottom of the bowl. Put the seeds into a colander, rinse under cool running water, and then pat dry. Preheat the oven and prepare the sheet pan as directed, then coat the seeds with the seasonings and spread them on the prepared pan. Roast, stirring once after about 10 minutes, until lightly toasted, about 18 minutes. These seeds have the hulls intact. You can eat them hull and all, or you can crack the hull with your teeth and eat the crispy seed inside—delicious either way.

CHILE COLORADO
con Carne y Papas

This comforting beef stew from northern Mexico is loaded with tender beef chuck and potatoes simmered in a homemade red chile sauce. It is also a common dish in New Mexico and El Paso. I like this classic served simply in a bowl with a side of charred corn tortillas, but it also goes well with soda bread (page 62) or flour tortillas, frijoles de la olla (page 24), and rice (page 285).

MAKES 12 SERVINGS

2 tablespoons olive oil

2 lb (1 kg) boneless beef chuck roast, cut into 1-inch (2.5-cm) cubes

4 cloves garlic, minced

3 russet potatoes, peeled and cut into 1-inch (2.5-cm) cubes

1 tablespoon all-purpose flour

2 cups (475 ml) Red Chile Sauce (page 17)

2 teaspoons tomato bouillon

1 teaspoon dried Mexican oregano

½ cup (120 ml) water, plus more if needed

Heat a large frying pan over medium-high heat. When the pan is hot, add the oil and swirl to coat the bottom. Add the beef and cook, turning as needed, until browned on all sides, about 5 minutes. Add the garlic and cook, stirring, until fragrant and softened, about 3 minutes. Stir in the potatoes, reduce the heat to low, cover, and cooking, stirring once or twice, until the potatoes are fork-tender and the meat is thoroughly cooked, about 15 minutes.

Uncover, increase the heat to medium, sprinkle the beef and potatoes with the flour, and cook, stirring, for 2 minutes. Pour in the chile sauce, add the bouillon and oregano, and stir well. Let the mixture come to a boil and then add the water. If the mixture seems too thick, add more water as needed to achieve a good consistency. Adjust the heat to maintain a gentle simmer and simmer, uncovered, for about 10 minutes to bring the flavors together. Serve hot.

SLOW-COOKER
Pot Roast

On special occasions, my grandma would fill and turn on her slow cooker early on a Sunday morning, and then after mass, the family would come to visit her and sit down to a late lunch. What often emerged from her slow cooker was a fall-apart-tender pot roast in a rich gravy with potatoes and carrots. This recipe is a warm and hearty meal that you can prepare with minimum effort, making it ideal for a weekday or weekend dinner.

MAKES 16 SERVINGS

1 boneless beef chuck roast, about 4 lb (1.8 kg)

2 teaspoons kosher salt

2 teaspoons ground black pepper

3 cloves garlic, sliced

1 teaspoon peppercorn medley

2 bay leaves, halved

1 cup (240 ml) unsalted beef broth

1 white onion, quartered

1 fresh rosemary sprig

4 large carrots, peeled and cut into 2-inch pieces

1 lb (450 g) small potatoes, halved

Flour or corn tortillas, warmed, for serving

Season the roast with the salt and pepper. Preheat a large frying pan over medium-high heat. Add the roast and sear, turning once, until a nice brown crust forms on both sides, about 3 minutes on each side.

Transfer the roast to a cutting board. Make 4 evenly spaced slits, each 2 inches (5 cm) deep, in the meat. Dividing them evenly, insert the garlic, peppercorns, and bay leaves into the slits.

Pour the broth into a slow cooker and then add the roast. Surround the roast with the onion quarters and set the rosemary sprig on top of the roast. Cover and cook on the low setting for 6 hours, adding the carrots and potatoes during the last 45 minutes of the cooking time. The meat should be fall-apart tender.

Taste and adjust the seasoning with salt if needed. To serve, slice or shred the meat, discarding the peppercorns and bay leaves, and arrange on a serving platter with the vegetables and gravy. Accompany with the tortillas.

CALABAZA
en Tacha

Make this traditional pumpkin dish as a side or a dessert. I have included it here in the Halloween section, but it is also a great addition to the Día de los Muertos or Thanksgiving table. If you can't find pumpkin, butternut squash is a good substitute.

MAKES 8 SERVINGS

1 pumpkin, 4–5 lb (1.8–2.3 kg)

2 cups (475 ml) water

3 cinnamon sticks

5 whole cloves

1 whole star anise pod

SPICED PILONCILLO SYRUP

¼ cup (60 ml) water

1 cinnamon stick

½ lb (225 g) piloncillo, chopped, or 1 cup (210 g) packed dark brown sugar

Whole milk or sweetened condensed milk, for serving

Rinse off the exterior of the pumpkin in cool or warm water, then, using a large serrated knife, cut the pumpkin in half through the stem end. Using a spoon, scoop out the pumpkin seeds and the stringy pulp layer. Discard the seeds (or save for roasting; see Cook's Note, page 191) and pulp. Cut the pumpkin into slices 3–4 inches (7.5–10 cm) thick, leaving the skin on.

In a large pot over high heat, combine the pumpkin, water, cinnamon, cloves, and star anise and bring to a boil. Reduce the heat to a simmer, cover tightly, and steam the pumpkin until tender, 20–40 minutes. The pumpkin is ready when a fork easily slides into the flesh.

While the pumpkin is steaming, make the syrup. In a small, heavy saucepan over very low heat, combine the water, cinnamon, and piloncillo and heat, stirring frequently, until the piloncillo dissolves and the syrup is smooth.

Serve the pumpkin slices topped with the syrup and in a pool of whole milk or drizzled with sweetened condensed milk. The skin softens during cooking and is also edible.

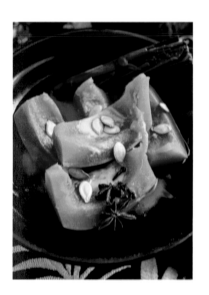

WITCHES' FINGERS
Sugar Cookies

These cookies are inspired by cookies my cousin Brenda made for Halloween one year and also for a Día de los Muertos celebration. They use a basic sugar cookie dough with hints of cinnamon and nutmeg and are shaped like witches' fingers, with fingernails made of roasted pepitas. They are wonderfully creepy and a great conversation starter. If you want the eating experience to be really spine-chilling, add a side of "bloody" berry sauce, using the berry filling from the Heart-Shaped Berry Empanadas (page 40) for dipping the fingers. Your kids will enjoy helping you make these scary treats.

MAKES ABOUT 24 COOKIES

3½ cups (435 g) all-purpose flour, plus more for dusting

1 teaspoon baking powder

½ teaspoon ground nutmeg

1 teaspoon ground cinnamon

1 cup (225 g) unsalted butter or margarine, at cool room temperature

1 cup (200 g) sugar

1 large egg

1 tablespoon pure vanilla extract

24 Spicy Roasted Pepitas (page 191) or sliced almonds

Unsweetened cocoa powder, for brushing

COOK'S NOTE: Don't worry about selecting perfect pepitas or almonds. The uglier the nails, the creepier the cookies.

In a medium bowl, whisk together the flour, baking powder, nutmeg, and cinnamon. In a large bowl, using an electric mixer, beat together the butter and sugar on medium speed until fluffy and light in color. Add the egg and vanilla and beat just until incorporated. On low speed, gradually add the flour mixture and beat until incorporated and the dough is not tacky to the touch. (It should be sticky but not stick to your fingers.)

Preheat the oven to 325°F (165°C). Line a large sheet pan with parchment paper.

On a lightly floured work surface, roll 1 tablespoon of the dough into a slender log 3–4 inches (7.5–10 cm) long. Make sure the log is slender, as the cookies will spread in the oven. To simulate a fingernail, gently press a pepita into one end of the log. Using fork tines, score the log crosswise to simulate knuckles. Transfer to the prepared sheet pan. Repeat with the remaining dough, spacing the logs about 1 inch (2.5 cm) apart.

Bake the cookies until the edges are just browned, 8–12 minutes. Let cool on the pan on a wire rack for 5 minutes. Using a pastry brush or a soft-bristled paintbrush, brush the knuckles with a little cocoa powder to make the hands look dirty and give them contrast, then transfer the cookies to the wire rack and let cool completely. The cookies will keep in an airtight container at room temperature for up to 1 week.

EL OJO

Whenever I was sick as a child, my mother did not take me to the doctor. Instead, she took me to my grandma's house. My grandma would diagnose me and heal me with natural *remedios* (remedies). If I was sick for no apparent reason she would say, "*Alguien te hizo mal de ojo*" (Someone gave you the evil eye). This cocktail, made with tequila, *agua fresca de tamarindo*, and bitters, is a nod to my grandma and all her caring natural *remedios*.

MAKES 1 COCKTAIL

2 fl oz (60 ml) tequila reposado

½ fl oz (15 ml) fresh lemon juice

1 fl oz (30 ml) Agua de Tamarindo (page 183)

1 egg white

Ice cubes

2 dashes Angostura bitters

1 fresh marigold, for garnish

In a cocktail shaker, combine the tequila, lemon juice, Agua de Tamarindo, and egg white, then fill the shaker two-thirds full with ice. Cover and shake vigorously until the outside of the shaker is lightly frosted.

Strain the mixture into a coupe glass. Add the bitters, garnish with the marigold, and serve.

Mal de ojo

DÍA DE LOS
Muertos
(Day of the Dead)

The local cemetery in the lower valley of El Paso was only a couple of blocks away from our home, and when I was little, I was scared of it. In retrospect, it wasn't scary at all. It is just old and quiet, and most of the plots are simple, marked with small stone barriers or wooden crosses. There are no trees or grass. It's just dirt.

I remember the day my grandma Jesusita held my hand and took me to the graveyard. She was carrying beautiful flowers from her garden, and we walked around the cemetery until she found her *angelitos* (little angels)—her two sons—who passed away within a month of each other. Jesús Manuel died before he was three years old, and Francisco died before he was one year old.

Grandma gently dusted off their grave plaque, and we placed the flowers on their graves. I asked my grandma how they died, and she got teary-eyed and didn't answer, so I never asked her again. I just knew that she loved them and missed them deeply, and visiting them was her way of remembering and feeling close to them. That was the day I stopped being afraid of the cemetery.

At the time, I didn't know why we were there on that chilly fall day. Now I realize that it must have been Día de los Muertos—Day of the Dead—the annual two-day holiday when people honor their departed loved ones. It falls on November 1 and 2, and November 1 is known as Día de los Inocentes (Day of the Innocents) or Día de los Angelitos (Day of the Little Angels). While the occasion might sound somber to people unfamiliar with it, Día de los Muertos is actually one of the brightest and most celebratory of all the Mexican holidays. It is also the day that I feel closest to my grandma, who left us many years ago.

Our family kicks off the holiday by creating a home altar, or *ofrenda*, on which are placed in full view photos of our dearly departed. Colorful *papel picado* (see page 108), bright yellow and orange marigolds, and hand-painted sugar skulls bring levity, reminding us that while we miss our loved ones, their lives enriched our world and we remain thankful for all that they gave us.

And as with all the best holidays, there's always lots of food. *Pan de muerto* is the traditional bread of the holiday, and I have included our family recipe, but I also like to make my grandma's favorite *pan dulces* (sweet breads), Conchas and Marranitos, to round out the basket. The holiday falls in mid-autumn, and Sopa de Verduras, which combines corn and squash blossoms, two longtime staples of the Mexican pantry, is the perfect seasonal soup. For a hearty main, I have included Chile Braised Pork Ribs, or you might try the traditional mole (page 289) in the Family Fiesta chapter. My grandma loved drinking *atoles*, warm corn flour–based drinks, so in this chapter, I am sharing recipes for a couple of our family's favorite flavors, strawberry and vanilla.

Although this holiday is traditionally Mexican, I encourage everyone to celebrate. What better way to honor our loved ones than by remembering them? You don't have to visit a graveyard to pay respect. You can instead make your own home altar (see page 205) to celebrate their lives. The recipes here are personal to my family, but you can make the dishes that remind you of your loved ones.

"Our dead are never dead to us, until we have forgotten them." —George Eliot

DAY OF THE DEAD
Altar

You do not have to create an elaborate Day of the Dead altar to honor your loved ones. But whether simple or sophisticated, altars—*ofrendas*—all have some basic elements in common: photographs of departed loved ones, belongings of the deceased, *papel picado* (see page 108), marigolds or other fresh flowers, incense, food and water or other beverage, religious symbols, sugar skulls (see page 226), and candles.

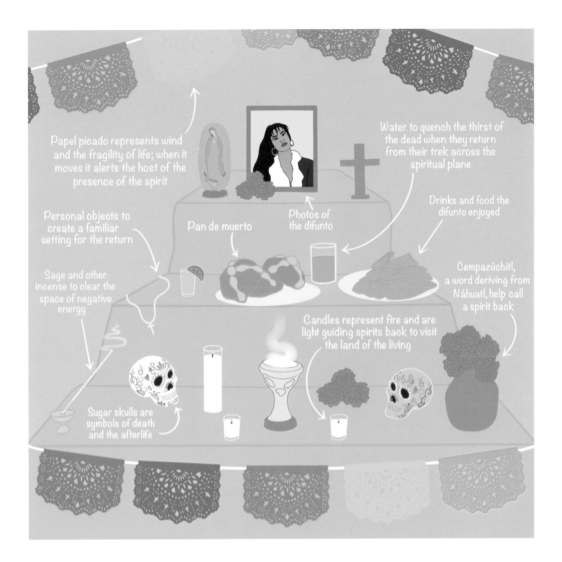

Papel picado represents wind and the fragility of life; when it moves it alerts the host of the presence of the spirit

Personal objects to create a familiar setting for the return

Sage and other incense to clear the space of negative energy

Pan de muerto

Photos of the difunto

Water to quench the thirst of the dead when they return from their trek across the spiritual plane

Drinks and food the difunto enjoyed

Cempazúchitl, a word deriving from Náhuatl, help call a spirit back

Candles represent fire and are light guiding spirits back to visit the land of the living

Sugar skulls are symbols of death and the afterlife

SPINACH &
Chile Verde Tortillas

Nothing beats the flavor of homemade corn tortillas. These tortillas are slightly spicy, tender, and soft. Make these green tortillas with pressed marigold petals to accompany Sopa de Verduras (page 208), or dress them up with a fresh spinach leaf or cilantro leaves for Saint Patrick's Day and use them for Corned Beef Brisket Tacos (page 58).

MAKES ABOUT FIFTEEN 5-INCH (13-CM) CORN TORTILLAS

2 cups (230 g) masa harina (corn flour)

½ teaspoon salt

⅓ cup (80 ml) cold water

1 cup (30 g) spinach leaves

1 jalapeño chile, roasted (page 15)

1 fresh Anaheim chile, roasted, peeled, and seeded (page 15)

1 poblano chile, roasted and peeled (page 15)

1 teaspoon olive oil

1 cup (240 ml) hot water

In a large bowl, whisk together the masa harina and salt.

In a blender, combine the cold water, spinach, and all the chiles and blend until puréed.

Pour the spinach-chile mixture into the masa harina, add the oil, and mix with your hands to combine. Gradually pour in the hot water while mixing constantly. If the mixture is too dry to come together, mix in warm water, a tablespoon at a time, until the masa (dough) comes together. If the dough is too wet, sprinkle it with a little masa harina and work it in. Knead the masa in the bowl until it is soft and smooth but not sticky, 2–3 minutes. It should have the texture of Play-Doh.

Divide the masa into 14–16 equal portions and shape each portion into a ball. Cover the balls with a kitchen towel so the masa does not dry out while you press the tortillas.

Preheat a comal (cast-iron griddle) or cast-iron frying pan over medium heat. Have ready a tortilla warmer or a basket lined with a kitchen towel.

When the comal is hot, open your tortilla press so the plates are flat and lay a piece of plastic wrap over each plate. Place a ball of masa on the center of the lower plate of the press, flatten it slightly with your hand, and then close the tortilla press and press down on the handle, flattening the masa into an even round. Open the press, peel off the plastic wrap covering the top of the tortilla, then lift the tortilla from the press with the bottom piece, flip the tortilla over onto your other hand, and peel off the second piece of plastic wrap.

COOK'S NOTES: If you do not have a tortilla press, lay a piece of plastic wrap on a work surface, top with a dough ball, flatten slightly, drape a second piece of plastic wrap over the dough ball, and then flatten into a thin, even round with a small, heavy frying pan.

If the tortillas are getting singed with black spots too quickly, reduce the heat slightly.

To decorate the tortillas with marigold petals, spinach leaves, or cilantro leaves, press the masa ball as directed, open the press, peel off the top piece of plastic wrap, evenly distribute the petals or leaves, re-cover with the plastic wrap, and press gently again to embed the petals or leaves in the tortilla.

Gently and carefully slide the tortilla off of your hand onto the hot comal and cook until the underside is freckled brown and the top is slightly puffy, about 30 seconds. Turn the tortilla over and cook until the second side is freckled brown, 20–30 seconds longer. Transfer the tortilla to the tortilla warmer or basket or simply wrap in a kitchen towel like my grandma kept her tortillas warm. Continue cooking the tortillas until all the masa balls are used.

If you will not be serving the tortillas right away, keep them warm wrapped in a kitchen towel and then in aluminum foil in a preheated 200°F (95°C) oven for up to 2 hours. Or you can let them cool, then refrigerate them in a resealable plastic bag for up to 3 days. To reheat, preheat a cast-iron frying pan over medium-high heat, then add the tortillas, one at a time, and heat for 15–30 seconds on each side.

SOPA
de Verduras

This *sopa de verduras*, or "vegetable soup," is economical, flavorful, and healthful and is perfect for anyone who has a vegetable garden or frequents farmers' markets with end-of-year harvest produce. This light, clear soup has floral notes that make it unique.

MAKES 6 SERVINGS

12 squash blossoms

2 tablespoons unsalted butter

½ cup (80 g) chopped yellow onion

2 cloves garlic, chopped

2 cups (340 g) fresh corn kernels

2 small green squashes or zucchini, chopped

8 cups (1.9 l) chicken broth

1 teaspoon fresh thyme leaves

1 teaspoon salt

½ teaspoon ground white or black pepper

Chopped fresh flat-leaf parsley and Mexican crema, for garnish (optional)

Remove the woody stems from the squash blossoms, then pluck out and discard the stamens (male flowers) and pistils (female flowers) from the centers of the blossoms. If they are fresh from the garden, be careful, as there might be bugs or bees inside! Trim off and discard the sepals (the small, wavy leaves that grow at the base of the blossoms). Cut each blossom into 4 equal pieces.

In a 4-quart (3.8-l) stockpot over medium heat, melt the butter. Add the onion and garlic and cook, stirring occasionally, until the onion is translucent, about 2 minutes. Add the corn kernels and squashes and continue to cook until the squashes become aromatic, 2–4 minutes. Add the broth, thyme, salt, and pepper, raise the heat to high, and bring to a boil. Reduce the heat to low, add the squash blossoms, and simmer until the vegetables are tender, about 10 minutes. Taste and adjust the seasoning with salt and pepper if needed.

Ladle the soup into individual bowls. Top with a scattering of parsley and a drizzle of crema, if using. Serve at once.

COOK'S NOTE: Cook the squash blossoms the day you pick or purchase them as they tend to wilt easily and lose their delicate shape and flavor. No squash blossoms? This soup is still delicious without them.

Para chuparse
los dedos

CHILE BRAISED
Pork Ribs

These chile-braised ribs are browned and then cooked low and slow for a couple of hours in my favorite red chile sauce and *chile de árbol*. I have added toasted árbol chiles to the sauce, which give it an earthy flavor with a hint of both smokiness and nuttiness. Serve these pork ribs with corn tortillas to sop up the sauce and a side of rice and beans for a hearty supper. Or shred the meat and serve it as a filling for tamales or tacos.

MAKES 12 SERVINGS

4 lb (1.8 kg) boneless country-style pork ribs

Salt and ground black pepper

2 tablespoons canola oil

4 dried árbol chiles, stemmed

1 small white onion, roughly chopped

3 cloves garlic, peeled

2 cups (475 ml) Red Chile Sauce (page 17)

1 cup (240 ml) vegetable, chicken, or pork broth, plus more if needed

Preheat a large (7–8-quart/6.6–7.6-l) Dutch oven or other heavy pot over medium-high heat. Generously sprinkle the pork ribs on all sides with salt and pepper. Add the oil to the hot pot and swirl to coat the bottom. Working in batches to avoid crowding the pot, add the ribs in a single layer and sear, turning as needed, until browned on all sides, 4–5 minutes total. As each batch is done, transfer it to a large plate.

In the same pot over medium heat, add the chiles, onion, and garlic and cook, stirring constantly, until all the ingredients are toasted, 1–2 minutes. The chiles should be well fried and change color, but watch them closely as they can burn easily. Remove from the heat.

Transfer the toasted chiles, onion, and garlic to a food processor or blender, add the chile sauce, and purée until smooth with specks of chile visible.

Meanwhile, return the pot to medium heat, add the broth, bring to a simmer, and deglaze the pot, stirring to dislodge any drippings and other browned bits stuck to the pot bottom.

Add the puréed sauce to the pot, season with ½ teaspoon each salt and pepper, and stir well. Nestle the pork ribs in the sauce and pour in any accumulated juices from the plate. Bring to a boil, reduce the heat to a simmer, cover, and simmer gently until the pork is fork-tender, 2½–3 hours. Check every now and again and add a little broth or water if the sauce is thickening too much.

Using a slotted spoon or tongs, transfer the pork ribs to a serving platter. Taste the sauce and adjust the seasoning with salt if needed, then ladle the sauce over the ribs and serve.

CAMOTES
Enmielados

This warm and comforting home-style dessert is not one you will see on the menu
at a Mexican restaurant. As the sweet potatoes, piloncillo, cinnamon, star anise,
and cloves simmer on the stove top, they give off a sweet and earthy aroma,
reminding you that fall has arrived. This dish is sweet but not rich and tastes similar
to traditional Thanksgiving yams but without the butter and marshmallows.
Although this recipe is perfect for Día de los Muertos, it will also add a nice Latin accent to
your Halloween or Thanksgiving menu.

MAKES 8 SERVINGS

6 cups (1.4 l) water

½ lb (225 g) piloncillo,
chopped, or 1 cup (210 g)
packed light brown sugar

2 cinnamon sticks

2 whole star anise pods

3 whole cloves

3 large sweet potatoes, peeled
and cut into slices 1 inch
(2.5 cm) thick

Whole milk or sweetened
condensed milk, for serving

In 3-quart (2.8-l) saucepan, over medium-high heat, combine the
water, piloncillo, cinnamon sticks, star anise, and cloves and bring
to a boil, stirring with a wooden spoon until the piloncillo dissolves.
Boil for 5 minutes, then add the sweet potatoes, reduce the heat
to a simmer, cover, and cook until the potatoes are tender, about
30 minutes. Remove and discard the cinnamon sticks, star anise,
and cloves.

Using a slotted spoon, transfer the potatoes to individual bowls. Top
with the warm syrup and a drizzle of milk and serve.

COOK'S NOTE: Pumpkin or winter squash, such as butternut
squash or Kubota, can be used in place of the sweet potatoes;
you will need about 1½ lb (680 g), peeled, seeded, and cut into
slices or wedges 1 inch (2.5 cm) thick.

PAN DE MUERTO

The signature food of Día de los Muertos, this round, pillowy Mexican bread, with hints
of citrus and anise, is crisscrossed with bread "bones" that symbolize the bones
of the deceased. This recipe makes three small loaves, so you can enjoy a loaf or two and
then place the third one on your home altar as a gift in honor of a departed loved
one. Serve a slice of this bread with a cup of *café de olla* (page 67) or Mexican Hot
Chocolate (page 277). I also like to use it for making French toast.

— ⁂ —

MAKES 3 SMALL LOAVES

½ cup (115 g) unsalted butter,
plus more for the sheet pan

½ cup (120 ml) whole milk

½ cup (120 ml) water

5–5½ cups (625–685 g) all-
purpose flour, plus more for
dusting

2 packages (2¼ teaspoons
each) active dry yeast

1 teaspoon salt

1 tablespoon aniseeds

½ cup (100 g) sugar

2 tablespoons pure orange
extract

Grated zest of 1 orange

4 large eggs

ORANGE GLAZE

½ cup (100 g) sugar

2 tablespoons grated orange
zest

⅓ cup (80 ml) fresh orange
juice

In a saucepan over medium heat, combine the butter, milk, and water
and heat just until the butter melts. Do not allow to boil.

In a large bowl, mix together ½ cup (65 g) of the flour, the yeast, salt,
aniseeds, and sugar. Using a whisk, slowly beat in the warm milk,
orange extract, and orange zest until well mixed. Add the eggs, one
at a time, beating well after each addition. Slowly add 1 cup (125 g)
of the flour while beating constantly. Continue slowly adding 1 cup
(125 g) of the flour at a time until the dough is soft but not sticky.
You may not need all the flour.

Turn the dough out onto a lightly floured work surface and knead
until smooth and elastic, at least 10 minutes. If the dough feels dry,
knead in more water, a teaspoon at a time. If the dough feels too wet,
knead in a little flour. Form the dough into a large ball and cut into
quarters. Shape each quarter into a smooth round loaf.

Lightly grease a large sheet pan with butter. Place 3 of the dough
balls on the pan, spacing them at least 3 inches (7.5 cm) apart.
Loosely cover the pan with plastic wrap or a kitchen towel and let the
balls rise in a warm place until doubled in size, 1–1½ hours.

Meanwhile, pinch off 3 pecan-sized pieces of dough from the fourth
ball and shape each piece into a small ball. Divide the leftover dough
into 6 equal pieces. On a lightly floured work surface, roll each
piece into a rope about 5 inches (13 cm) long. (They need to be long
enough form a cross over the top and down the sides of each loaf.)
Spread out your index, middle, and ring finger and use them to roll
and press indentations into each dough rope to simulate bumpy
bones. Place the "bones" and the 3 small balls on a plate or small
sheet pan, cover loosely with plastic wrap, and refrigerate to slow the
rising process.

Continues on the following page

Continued from the previous page

COOK'S NOTE: If you like, replace the orange glaze with a simple butter topping. As soon as the loaves are removed from the oven, brush the tops with melted butter and then sprinkle with granulated sugar, colored sanding sugar, grated Mexican chocolate, ground cinnamon, or marigold petals.

Once the loaves have risen, preheat the oven to 350°F (180°C). Lightly brush the top of each loaf with water and lay two "bones" across the loaf and down the sides, forming a cross and pressing gently to adhere. On each loaf, using your index finger, gently press where the "bones" intersect on top, forming a dimple. Lightly brush each dimple with water and place a small dough ball in the dimple, pressing gently so it adheres.

Bake the loaves until lightly browned and they sound hollow when thumped on the bottom, 25–30 minutes.

While the loaves are baking, make the orange glaze. In a saucepan over medium heat, combine the sugar, orange zest, and orange juice and bring just to a boil, stirring until the sugar dissolves. Remove from the heat.

When the loaves are ready, let cool on the pan on a wire rack for a few minutes, then brush the loaves with the glaze. Let the glaze set for a few minutes, then transfer the loaves to the rack and let cool completely before slicing and serving.

HORCHATA & MEXICAN CHOCOLATE *Conchas*

A *concha* is a soft and sweet Mexican bread topped with a sweet crust that crumbles easily. *Concha* means "seashell" in Spanish, and the crust of these small breads is layered to look like their name. White (vanilla) and brown (chocolate) are the classic toppings. The two toppings here are inspired by the flavors of horchata and Mexican chocolate. I use bread flour for the dough and leave it to rise overnight in the refrigerator, which results in an airy texture. For the best result, have the milk, eggs, and butter at room temperature before you begin making the dough.

MAKES 12 SMALL BREADS

DOUGH

4 cups (500 g) bread flour, plus more for dusting

3½ teaspoons instant yeast

½ cup (100 g) granulated sugar

1½ teaspoons salt

1 cup plus 2 tablespoons (265 ml) whole milk, at room temperature

2 large eggs, at room temperature

2 teaspoons pure vanilla extract

½ cup (115 g) unsalted butter, at room temperature, cut into small chunks, plus more for the bowl and for rubbing on the shaped breads

Continues on the following page

To make the dough, in a large bowl, whisk together the bread flour, yeast, granulated sugar, and salt. In a medium bowl, whisk together the milk, eggs, and vanilla until blended. Slowly add the milk mixture to the flour mixture while mixing constantly with a wooden spoon. Add the butter chunks and continue to mix until a rough dough forms that comes away from the sides of the bowl. This is a very sticky and wet dough. Resist the temptation to add more flour to it. Turn the dough out onto a floured work surface and knead it just enough to shape it into a smooth, elastic ball, about 2 minutes. (You can also make this dough in a stand mixer. Mix the dough with the dough hook attachment on medium speed for about 7 minutes.)

Lightly butter a second large bowl. Place the dough in the bowl, cover the bowl with plastic wrap, and refrigerate overnight.

To make the toppings, sift together the all-purpose flour and confectioners' sugar into a bowl. Add the butter and vanilla extract and mix with a rubber spatula until fully combined and soft.

Divide the mixture in half and place each half in a separate small bowl. Add the cinnamon and cloves to 1 bowl and mix well, then add the cocoa powder and chocolate to the second bowl and mix well. Wrap the toppings separately in plastic wrap and refrigerate until needed.

Continued from the previous page

TOPPINGS

1 cup (125 g) all-purpose flour

1 cup (115 g) confectioners' sugar

½ cup plus 2 tablespoons (145 g) unsalted butter or solid vegetable shortening, at room temperature

2½ teaspoons pure vanilla extract

2 teaspoons ground cinnamon

¼ teaspoon ground cloves

1 tablespoon unsweetened cocoa powder

1 teaspoon grated Mexican chocolate

To shape the breads, lightly dust a work surface with flour. Remove the dough from the refrigerator and turn it out onto the floured surface. Divide into 12 equal portions, cover with a kitchen towel, and let come to room temperature for about 15 minutes. Meanwhile line 2 sheet pans with parchment paper.

Shape each dough portion into a ball and place the balls on the prepared sheet pans, dividing them evenly between the pans and spacing them about 2 inches (5 cm) apart. Using your palm, push lightly on each ball to flatten slightly into a round. Soften some butter with your hands and coat the surface of each round bun evenly.

To cover the rounds with the toppings, divide each topping into 6 equal portions (about 2 tablespoons each). Lightly knead a portion until pliable, then, using a rolling pin, roll it out into a thin round, drape it over a dough round, and pat down lightly to adhere. Repeat until all the dough rounds are topped. Using a sharp paring knife, lame (double-sided dough scoring tool), or a traditional concha cutter, cut grooves in the topping to simulate the pattern of a clamshell. Or you can decorate the topping with other types of cuts, such as circles or crisscrosses. As you work, be careful to score only the topping. Do not cut into the dough. Cover with a kitchen towel and let rise until nearly doubled in size, 30–45 minutes. About 15 minutes before they are ready, preheat the oven to 350°F (180°C).

Bake the conchas until golden brown, 18–22 minutes. Transfer to wire racks to cool. Serve warm or at room temperature. Conchas are best the day they are baked, but leftovers will keep in an airtight container at room temperature for up to 3 days.

MARRANITOS
(Pig-Shaped Cookies)

Marranitos (little pigs)—or *cochinitos* or *puerquitos*, as they are called in some Mexican American communities—were my grandma's favorite sweet bread and remind me so much of her. When I was growing up, we never made them at home. Instead, we bought them at the nearby *panadería* (Mexican bakery). Not everyone has a local *panadería*, however, and this iconic Mexican sweet bread, with its lightly spiced flavor and its cake-like texture reminiscent of shortbread, is easy to make at home. *Marranitos* are often called gingerbread pigs, even though they contain only a small amount of the spice. Their signature deep, rich flavor comes from the addition of both molasses and *piloncillo*.

MAKES EIGHTEEN 6-INCH (15-CM) COOKIES

4 tablespoons (60 g) unsalted butter or solid vegetable shortening, at room temperature

1¼ cups (270 g) packed grated piloncillo or dark brown sugar

1 large egg, at room temperature

⅓ cup (80 ml) whole milk

1½ teaspoons vanilla bean paste or pure vanilla extract

1½ teaspoons baking soda

1½ teaspoons ground cinnamon

1 teaspoon ground ginger

¾ cup (255 g) molasses

¼ cup (85 g) honey

5–6 cups (625–750 g) all-purpose flour, plus more for the cutter

1 large egg beaten with 1 tablespoon water, for the egg wash

In a large bowl, using an electric mixer, beat together the butter and piloncillo on medium speed until creamy and smooth. Add the egg, milk, and vanilla and beat again until smooth. Add the baking soda, cinnamon, ginger, molasses, and honey and beat until thoroughly incorporated.

On low speed, beat in 3 cups (375 g) of the flour until incorporated. Gradually add the remaining flour, switching from the mixer to a wooden spoon once the dough becomes very stiff (so you don't burn out your mixer motor). The dough will seem crumbly, so once you've stirred in as much of the flour as you can, use your hands to quickly knead in the rest of the flour and bring the dough together. You're looking for a dough that is firm enough to roll out. You may not need all the flour.

Lay a sheet of plastic wrap on a work surface and turn the dough out onto it. Divide the dough in half, form each half into a thick disk, and wrap each disk in plastic wrap. Refrigerate for at least 1 hour or for up to 2 days.

Preheat the oven to 350°F (180°C). Line 2 sheet pans with parchment paper.

Remove a dough disk from the refrigerator and cut it in half. Rewrap half and return it to the refrigerator. Lay a sheet of plastic wrap on a work surface, place the remaining disk half in the center, and then

COOK'S NOTE: You can use pig-shaped cutters in different sizes, and if you don't have a pig-shaped cutter, you can use a cutter in any shape you like. You can also substitute dark corn syrup, honey, or maple syrup for the molasses.

top with a second sheet of plastic wrap. Roll out the dough ¼ inch (6 mm) thick. Using a 6-inch pig-shaped cookie cutter, dip it into flour and then cut out as many cookies as possible, dipping the cutter into flour before each cut. Transfer the cutouts to a prepared sheet pan, spacing them 1 inch (2.5 cm) apart. Gather up the dough scraps and set aside. Repeat with the remaining disk half. Then press together the dough scraps and repeat the rolling and cutting. Now repeat with the remaining dough disk, first cutting it in half and then rolling and cutting each half. Lightly brush the cookies with the egg wash.

Bake the cookies until they start to turn golden around the edges and the center appears dry, 9–12 minutes. Transfer the cookies to wire racks to cool completely. If you have made smaller cookies, they will be crunchier. The cookies will keep layered between sheets of waxed paper in an airtight container at room temperature for up to 3 days or in the freezer for up to 3 months.

ATOLE

Thickened with corn flour and served warm, *atoles* are the quintessential cold-weather breakfast drink, often paired with sweet tamales, and are also served during fall and winter fiestas. They are made in many flavors, with vanilla and strawberry being two of our family favorites.

———— ꞛ•ꞛ ————

Atole de Vainilla

MAKES 6 SERVINGS

2½ cups (600 ml) water

1 cinnamon stick

¼ lb (115 g) piloncillo, chopped, or ½ cup (100 g) packed dark brown sugar

¼ cup (30 g) masa harina (corn flour)

2 cups (475 ml) whole milk

1 vanilla bean, split lengthwise

Ground cinnamon, for sprinkling (optional)

In a large saucepan over medium-high heat, combine the water, cinnamon stick, and piloncillo and bring to a boil, stirring to dissolve the sugar. Remove from the heat, cover, and let steep for about 30 minutes.

Remove and discard the cinnamon stick and return the pan to low heat. While whisking constantly, slowly add the masa harina, continuing to whisk until fully dissolved. Pour in the milk. Then, using the tip of a knife, scrape the seeds from the vanilla bean halves and add to the pan. Raise the heat to medium and bring the mixture just to a boil. Reduce the heat to low and simmer uncovered, whisking occasionally, for 20 minutes to blend the flavors.

Serve at once, sprinkled with ground cinnamon, if desired.

Atole de Fresa

MAKES 6 SERVINGS

1½ cups (350 ml) water

1 cinnamon stick

6 strawberries, stemmed and halved

2 tablespoons masa harina (corn flour)

3 cups (700 ml) whole milk

Pinch of baking soda

¼ cup (50 g) sugar

In a small saucepan over medium-high heat, combine 1 cup (240 ml) of the water, the cinnamon stick, and the strawberries and bring to a boil. Reduce the heat to a gentle simmer and simmer for 5 minutes.

Using tongs or a slotted spoon, transfer the strawberries to a blender, then add 1 tablespoon of the liquid from the pan and purée until smooth. Discard the cinnamon stick and the remaining water in the pan. Reserve the blended strawberries.

In a measuring pitcher, whisk together the masa harina and the remaining ½ cup (120 ml) water to make a slurry. Set aside.

In a large saucepan over medium-high heat, combine the milk and baking soda. Bring to just below a boil, then stir in the strawberries and the slurry, mixing well. Reduce the heat to low, stir in the sugar, and simmer, stirring often, until the sugar dissolves and the mixture thickens to the desired consistency. Serve at once.

BLOOD ORANGE
Marigold Margarita

Tart blood orange juice makes a brilliantly colored—not to mention very uplifting—cocktail. For a touch of Día de los Muertos spirit, sweeten the margaritas with a homemade *cempasúchil* (marigold) syrup for floral, citrusy, and sweet notes.

— ❦ · ❧ —

MAKES 2 COCKTAILS

Coarse salt, 4–5 dried marigold flowers, and lime wedge, for the glass rim

Ice cubes

Juice of 3 blood oranges

Juice of 2 limes

4 fl oz (120 ml) tequila blanco or mezcal

2 fl oz (60 ml) cempasúchil syrup (see Cook's Note) or triple sec

2 blood orange slices, for garnish

Pour a layer of salt onto a small, flat plate, crumble the flowers into the salt, and mix together. Run the lime wedge around the rim of a cocktail glass, then roll the outer rim in the salt-marigold mixture, coating it evenly. Repeat with a second cocktail glass. Fill the glasses with ice and set aside.

In a cocktail shaker, combine the orange juice, lime juice, tequila, and cempasúchil syrup and fill the shaker two-thirds full with ice. Cover and shake vigorously until the outside of the shaker is lightly frosted.

Strain the mixture into the prepared glasses. Garnish each glass with an orange slice and serve.

COOK'S NOTE: To make cempasúchil (marigold syrup), in a blender, combine the petals of 8 fresh marigolds and 2 cups (475 ml) simple syrup (see Cook's Note, page 225) and blend on medium speed until smooth. Strain through a fine-mesh sieve set over a bowl and discard the solids in the sieve. The syrup will keep in an airtight container in the refrigerator for up to 1 month.

MOCKTAIL MARGARITA: Omit the tequila, shake up the citrus juices with the cempasúchil syrup, and top off each cocktail with blood orange soda or sparkling water for some fizz.

Sugar Skulls

It is important to make sugar skulls for your Día de los Muertos celebration because they represent your departed loved ones. They are easy to assemble and fun to decorate. Look for sugar skull molds in large chain department stores catering to Mexican American shoppers, in Mexican American shops, and online. You can also purchase decorating kits.

MAKES 2 MEDIUM-SIZE FLAT-BACK SUGAR SKULLS AND 1 LARGE TWO-SIDED SKULL

1 cup (200 g) sugar

2–3 teaspoons meringue powder

2–3 teaspoons water

1 medium-size sugar skull mold, about 3¼ by 2¼ by 1½ inches (8 by 5.5 by 4 cm)

1 large two-part sugar skull mold, about 4½ by 4 by 4½ inches (11. 5 by 10 by 11.5 cm)

4 cardboard squares, at least 2 inches (5 cm) larger than the molds

Ready-to-use royal icing

Decorations of choice

In a large bowl, whisk together the sugar and meringue powder until well mixed. Sprinkle 2 teaspoons of the water over the sugar mixture, then mix with your hands until the mixture is the consistency of thick, wet sand and holds together when you squeeze it. If it seems a bit dry, add a little more water.

Fill the medium-size skull mold with some of the sugar mixture, packing it tightly. Scrape off any excess mixture so the skull will have a smooth, flat back when unmolded. Press a cardboard square onto the back of the mold and flip the mold and cardboard over. You should be able to lift the mold easily off to reveal a perfectly shaped sugar skull. Repeat to make a second medium-size skull. Then, using the two-part large skull mold, fill and unmold both parts the same way. Let all the skulls dry at least overnight or for 24 hours.

To make the large two-sided skull, spread a thin layer of royal icing on the back of the front of the skull and press the back of the skull against it. Carefully remove any excess icing from around the seam, then set aside for at least 30 minutes to allow the icing to dry and bind the two halves together.

Once dry, your sugar skulls are ready to decorate with royal icing (use food coloring to create a variety of icing colors), small pompoms, glitter, colored foils, rhinestones, feathers—whatever you like—using the icing as your glue.

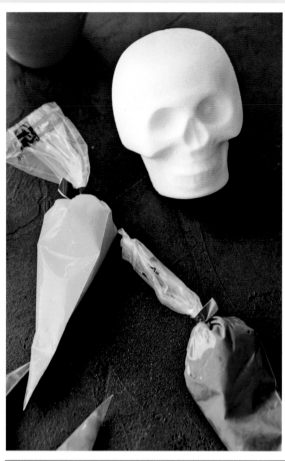

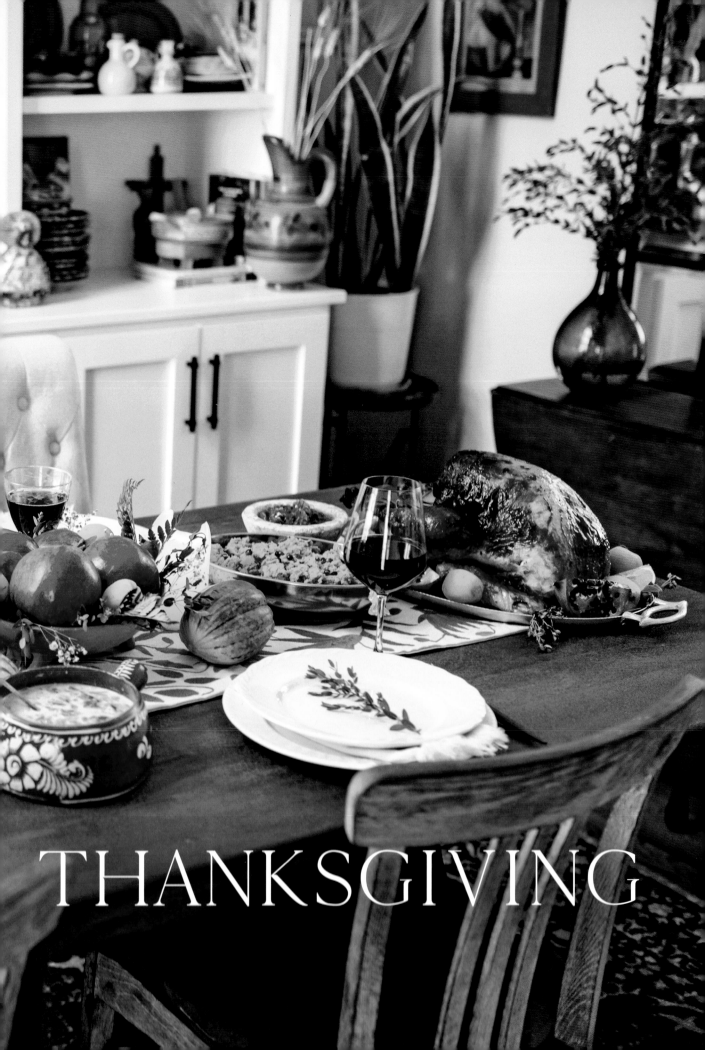

THANKSGIVING

Thanksgiving is easily one of my favorite holidays of the year. The focus is always on food and on expressing gratefulness, which makes it the perfect kickoff to the hectic winter holiday season.

As they say, some like it hot, and in *nuestra familia*, we are definitely among those who do like spice for Thanksgiving. Of course, at the heart of the celebration is the traditional turkey day spread. We just like to spice it up with some fun Mexican twists! We usually host a late Thanksgiving lunch around two and then we graze all day and eat round two for dinner at six. Our family fiestas are usually casual and buffet style, but on Thanksgiving, the prettiest dishes are set out and we all squeeze around the dinner table—or tables, depending on the crowd size—and eat at the same time.

When I'm in charge of the bird, the centerpiece of the Thanksgiving table is Pavo Enchilado, a sweet and spicy take on roasted turkey. There is also Mexican chorizo in the stuffing and smoky chipotles in the sweet potatoes, which give the standard menu a strong Mexican accent.

A dish of Rajas con Queso, which marries roasted green chiles, onion, buttermilk, and asadero cheese, is always on the table. It makes a rich, melty vegetarian appetizer with tortilla chips, is great dolloped on roasted turkey, or is a delicious filling for tamales after the holiday. Traditional Mexican *bolillos*, crusty on the outside and soft on the inside, replace more common dinner rolls, and festive sangria flows freely to keep spirits high.

Guests typically want to contribute to the menu, so I focus on the savory side and give everyone else license to bring their cakes, pies, cookies, and more. The dessert bar is always a fun compilation of everyone's favorite sweets. Nothing could make me happier than this meshing of our traditional savory offerings with their time-honored desserts.

Of course, as a firm believer that more is *always* more when it comes to food-themed holidays, we invariably have tons of leftovers. To keep the menu fresh, we turn our leftovers into a taco and *torta* (sandwich) bar, complete with salsas and spreads that help breathe new life into the Thanksgiving Day surplus.

Honestly, what's better than extending the celebration well into the long weekend? After all the Black Friday shopping and football watching, there are lots of hungry tummies to fill. We call the day after the main meal our Thanksgiving Fiesta, Part Dos!

BOLILLOS

If you are from El Paso, these are called *francesitos*. I'm guessing the name came from *pan francés* (French bread), but because they are smaller than a full-size loaf, they were dubbed *francesitos*. Some people think that's funny because *francesitos* literally translates to "little French men."

These rolls are lightly crunchy on the outside and pillowy on the inside. They can be served as is or split lengthwise to make *tortas* (sandwiches) or *molletes*, open-face sandwiches that are traditionally buttered, slathered with refried beans, topped with cheese, and then baked until the cheese melts and the bread is crispy.

MAKES 8 ROLLS

3¾ cups (470 g) all-purpose flour, plus more for dusting

1 package (2¼ teaspoons) active dry yeast

1 tablespoon sugar

¾ teaspoon salt

1½ cups (350 ml) lukewarm water (120–130°F/49°–54°C)

Vegetable oil, for the bowl

In a large bowl, whisk together 1½ cups (190 g) of the flour, the yeast, sugar, and salt. Pour in the water and beat with an electric mixer on low to medium speed for 30 seconds, stopping to scrape down the sides of the bowl as needed. Increase the speed to high and beat for 3 minutes. Then, using a wooden spoon, stir in as much of the remaining flour as you can.

Turn the dough out onto a lightly floured work surface and knead, working in more of the remaining flour as needed, until you have a moderately stiff dough that is smooth and elastic, 6–8 minutes. You may not need all the flour. Shape the dough into a ball. Lightly oil a large bowl, add the dough, and then turn the dough to coat the entire surface with oil. Cover the bowl with a kitchen towel and let the dough rise in a warm place until doubled in size, about 1 hour.

Line a large sheet pan with parchment paper. Punch down the dough, then turn it out onto a lightly floured surface and cut it into 8 equal pieces. Roll each piece into a ball and place on the prepared sheet pan, spacing them 2 inches (5 cm) apart. Lightly brush or spray with water and let rise, uncovered, for 10 minutes.

On a lightly floured work surface, shape each dough ball into a chubby, slightly tapered oval roll about 6 inches (15 cm) long, modestly tapering both ends. As each roll is shaped, return it to the sheet pan, again spacing the rolls about 2 inches (5 cm) apart.

Lightly brush or spray the shaped rolls with water so they will not dry out, then cover with a kitchen towel and let rise in a warm place until puffy, 30–45 minutes. About 20 minutes before the rise is over, preheat the oven to 400°F (200°C).

When ready to bake, lightly brush or spray the rolls with water one more time. Using a razor blade or lame (double-sided dough scoring tool), score each roll with a single long slash from end to end about ¼ inch (6 mm) deep. The dough may deflate a bit, but that's okay. It will puff right up in the hot oven.

Bake the rolls until golden brown, 20–22 minutes. Transfer to wire racks and let cool completely. The rolls are best if eaten the day they are baked, but they will keep tightly wrapped in a sealed plastic bag at room temperature for 2 days.

CHIPOTLE
Mashed Sweet Potatoes

This fall side dish marries sweet potatoes with orange juice and zest for a hint of citrus, yogurt and butter for a smooth and creamy consistency, and *piloncillo* and chipotle chiles for a sweet and spicy kick. It is a natural addition to a Thanksgiving menu, but it is also quick and easy enough to make whenever you crave bold, complex flavors in a single dish.

— ❧ • ❧ —

MAKES 6–8 SERVINGS

5 tablespoons (75 g) unsalted butter, plus more for the baking dish

4 sweet potatoes, about 2 lb (1 kg) total weight, peeled and cut into 1-inch (2.5-cm) cubes

Grated zest of 1 orange

¼ cup (60 ml) fresh orange juice

½ cup (100 g) plain Greek yogurt

2 chipotle chiles in adobo sauce, minced, plus 1 tablespoon adobo sauce

¼ cup (60 g) packed grated piloncillo or dark brown sugar

1 teaspoon pure vanilla extract

1 teaspoon salt

Pomegranate seeds, for garnish

Preheat the oven to 350°F (180°C). Butter an 8-inch (20-cm) square oven-to-table baking dish.

In a large saucepan or a stockpot over high heat, combine the sweet potatoes with water to cover and bring to a boil. Reduce the heat to medium and cook, uncovered, until tender, 10–15 minutes. Drain the potatoes into a colander and then return them to the pan.

Add the orange zest and juice, yogurt, 3 tablespoons of the butter, chipotle chiles and adobo sauce, piloncillo, vanilla, and salt to the potatoes. Using a potato masher, mash the potatoes, mixing them well with all the other ingredients, until smooth.

Spoon the potato mixture into the prepared baking dish, spreading it evenly. Cut the remaining 2 tablespoons butter into small bits and dot the top. Bake the potatoes until heated through and the top is slightly darker, about 20 minutes.

Remove from the oven, sprinkle with the pomegranate seeds, and serve hot.

COOK'S NOTE: The sweet potato mixture can be made up to 3 days in advance, spooned into the buttered baking dish, covered, and refrigerated. Bake directly from the refrigerator in a preheated 350°F (180°C) oven until heated through, 30–35 minutes. Serve as directed.

RAJAS
con Queso

My grandma always made this delicious staple to eat with *frijoles de la olla* (page 24). The combination of buttermilk and Mexican *crema* gives the green chiles a creamy tang and perfect saltiness. The last time my grandma made this dish for the family was for our last Thanksgiving celebration with her, two months before she passed away in 2003. On that day, my mom roasted the chiles, and Grandma, who was seated in her wheelchair at the kitchen table—where she always loved to be—peeled off the skins. Our family now makes this dish every Thanksgiving in her honor. It is a great appetizer accompanied with chips and is also delicious served over turkey and mashed potatoes. This is our "gravy"—and it is beyond rich and addicting.

MAKES 12 SERVINGS

2 tablespoons olive oil

½ cup (80 g) chopped white onion

1 tablespoon all-purpose flour

5 cups (1.2 kg) roasted, peeled, seeded, and cut-up fresh Anaheim or Hatch chiles, in 1-inch (2.5-cm) pieces (page 15)

1–2 jalapeño chiles, roasted, peeled, seeded, and chopped (page 15, optional; for extra spice)

½ cup (120 ml) Mexican crema

2 cups (475 ml) buttermilk

2 tablespoons garlic powder

2½ cups (285 g) shredded asadero, quesadilla, or Muenster cheese

Salt

In a large frying pan over medium heat, warm the oil. Add the onion and cook, stirring often, until translucent, about 2 minutes. Add the flour and stir for 2 minutes. Add the Anaheim chiles and the jalapeños, if using, and cook, stirring constantly, for 2 minutes to bring all the flavors together.

Add the crema, buttermilk, and garlic powder and bring to a boil. Stir in the cheese, cover, and remove from the heat. Allow the cheese to melt completely before serving. The mixture should thicken slightly. If it is too thick, add a little water to thin. Then season to taste with salt and serve.

CHORIZO & BACON
Stuffing

My mom makes the absolute best stuffing for Thanksgiving. This recipe
is similar to hers, but it has fewer ingredients and is a bit easier to make.
The flavors of the chorizo and bacon really make this stuffing shine.

MAKES 12 SERVINGS

1-lb (450 g) loaf white
sandwich bread

9 oz (250 g) Mexican pork
chorizo

1 lb (450 g) sliced bacon

¾ cup (110 g) finely chopped
white onion

4 cups (950 ml) low-sodium
chicken broth, plus more if
needed

¾ cup (170 g) unsalted butter,
plus more for the baking dish

2 carrots, peeled and shredded
in a food processor fitted with
the grater blade

4 celery ribs, quartered and
shredded in a food processor
fitted with the grater blade

1 tablespoon chopped fresh
sage

1 tablespoon dried Mexican
oregano

1 teaspoon ground black
pepper

¼ teaspoon salt

Nonstick cooking spray,
for the foil

Preheat the oven to 350°F (180°C). Cut the bread into 1-inch
(2.5-cm) cubes. Spread the bread pieces on a large sheet pan and
toast, turning once, until lightly golden, about 5 minutes on each
side. Set aside.

If the chorizo is in a casing, discard the casing. Crumble the
chorizo into a medium frying pan and cook over medium-low
heat, breaking up the meat and stirring often, until evenly cooked,
about 10 minutes. Set aside.

Chop the bacon with a knife or snip with kitchen shears into ½-inch
(12-mm) pieces. Line a large plate with paper towels and set it near
the stove. In a large frying pan over medium heat, fry the bacon,
stirring occasionally, until cooked but not crispy, about 5 minutes.
Using a slotted spoon, transfer the bacon to the towel-lined plate to
drain and set aside. Pour off all but a small spoonful of the drippings
from the pan.

Return the pan to medium-high heat, add the onion, and cook,
stirring often, until tender, 5–7 minutes. Add the cooked chorizo and
cooked bacon, stir together with the onion, and cook, stirring, for a
few minutes to allow the flavors to come together. Remove from the
heat and set aside to cool.

In a saucepan over medium heat, combine the broth, ½ cup (115 g)
of the butter, the carrots, and the celery and heat just until the butter
melts. Remove from the heat.

In a large bowl, combine the toasted bread pieces, the bacon-chorizo
mixture, and the broth mixture and stir until the bread is evenly
moistened and all the ingredients are evenly distributed. If the
mixture seems too dry, add more broth, a little at a time. The mixture
should be moist but not soggy.

Add the sage, oregano, pepper, and salt and mix well. Cover and refrigerate overnight to allow the flavors to blend.

Preheat the oven to 350°F (180°C). Butter a 9 x 11-inch (23 x 28-cm) baking pan or dish.

Transfer the stuffing to the prepared baking pan, spreading it evenly. Cut the remaining 4 tablespoons (55 g) butter into pats and lay them on top, spacing them evenly. Spray a sheet of aluminum foil large enough to cover the pan with cooking spray and cover the pan, sprayed side down.

Bake the stuffing for 45 minutes. Uncover and continue to bake until golden brown and bubbling, about 10 minutes longer. Serve hot.

PAVO ENCHILADO

Give your turkey dinner a Latin twist with this inspired roast turkey recipe. First, you'll fill the cavity with aromatics and an orange. Next, you'll rub a mixture of apricot preserves and butter underneath the skin and all over the outside of the bird, adding both sweetness and richness. Finally, you'll inject red chile sauce into the flesh, which creates a marbled effect and yields loads of flavor. After time in the oven, the bird will emerge bronzed and beautiful.

— ❧ • ❧ —

MAKES 8–10 SERVINGS

1 turkey, 12–14 lb (5.4–6.4 kg)

1 orange, halved

1 white onion, coarsely chopped

3 cloves garlic, peeled

⅔ oz (20 g) poultry herb blend

½ cup (140 g) apricot preserves

3 tablespoons unsalted butter, at room temperature

3 cups (700 ml) Red Chile Sauce (page 17)

Salt and ground black pepper

4 cups (950 ml) chicken broth

Remove the turkey from its packaging. Locate the neck and giblets package inside the body cavity, remove them, and reserve for another use (see Cook's Note).

Place the turkey, breast side up, on a rack in a large roasting pan. Tuck the wing tips under the turkey body. Fill the body cavity with the orange halves, onion, garlic, and herbs.

In a small bowl, mix together the apricot preserves and butter. Starting at the cavity, carefully slide your fingers between the skin and the breast meat, loosening the skin. Then spread a thin layer of the butter-preserves mixture over the meat. Pat the skin back in place. Rub the remaining butter-preserves mixture all over the turkey, covering it evenly.

Using a meat injector, inject 1 cup (240 ml) of the chile sauce into the turkey, spacing the injections evenly over the breasts and thighs and injecting about 4 tablespoons at each location. Drizzle the turkey evenly with the remaining chile sauce. Season the turkey generously with salt and pepper. Cover the turkey loosely with aluminum foil and let sit at room temperature for 30 minutes. (Alternatively, you can refrigerate the turkey overnight; remove the turkey from the refrigerator about 30 minutes before you are ready to roast it.)

Preheat the oven to 450°F (230°C). When the oven is ready, pour the broth into the roasting pan. Cover the turkey loosely with aluminum foil. Slide the pan into the oven and reduce the oven temperature to 350°F (180°C). Roast the turkey, rotating the pan back to front every hour for even roasting, until an instant-read thermometer inserted into thickest part of a thigh away from bone registers 165°F (74°C), about 2¾–3 hours.

Transfer the turkey to a large platter and let rest for at least 20 minutes before carving.

COOK'S NOTES: If I could give you only one piece of advice, it would be to be sure you remove the neck and the package of giblets from the turkey cavity before cooking the bird. Dig deep, as sometimes they are a bit hidden. You can save the giblets, neck, and drippings from roasted turkey for making a giblet gravy.

No roasting rack? Arrange celery ribs in a rack pattern on the bottom of the roasting pan and set the turkey on top.

To calculate how long it takes to roast a turkey in a 350°F (180°C) oven, plan on 13 minutes per pound (450 g), or about 3 hours for a turkey weighing 14 pounds (6.4 kg).

EMPANADAS
de Camote

My grandma often bought sweet potatoes and used them to make a dessert rather than a savory dish. She would make empanadas with whatever was in season, and her sweet potato empanadas were a special treat. Because an empanada is a handheld pie, it is a perfect dessert after a Thanksgiving feast—no dishes or utensils needed. This classic filling is flavored with *piloncillo* and warm fall spices. I have given the dough a modern touch with the addition of beer and butter, which results in a particularly light, flaky, and flavorful pastry.

MAKES 14 EMPANADAS

FILLING

1 cup (240 ml) water

½ lb (225 g) piloncillo, chopped, or 1 cup (210 g) packed dark brown sugar

1 cinnamon stick

3 whole cloves

3 sweet potatoes, about 1½ lb (680 g) total weight

DOUGH

3⅓ cups (415 g) all-purpose flour

3 tablespoons granulated sugar

1 teaspoon ground cinnamon

1 teaspoon salt

¾ cup (170 g) butter, at room temperature

1 large egg

½ cup (120 ml) dark beer, at room temperature

1 large egg beaten with 2 tablespoons water, for the egg wash

To prepare the filling, in a small saucepan over high heat, combine the water, piloncillo, cinnamon, and cloves and bring to a boil, stirring to dissolve the piloncillo. Remove from the heat, cover, and let steep for 30 minutes.

Meanwhile, pierce each sweet potato with a fork two or three times. Place the potatoes on a microwave-safe plate and microwave until soft and tender, 10–15 minutes. If they are too firm, continue to cook them in the microwave in 1-minute increments. Let the potatoes cool until they can be handled, then peel and discard the skins.

Put the potatoes into a bowl. Using a potato masher, mash the potatoes while adding the piloncillo syrup, a little at a time, until you have a whipped consistency. You may not need to use all the syrup. Cover and refrigerate the filling until cold.

To make the dough, in a bowl, whisk together the flour, sugar, cinnamon, and salt. In a stand mixer fitted with the dough hook, beat the butter on medium-low speed until creamy. Add the egg and beat until well mixed. With the mixer on low speed, add the flour mixture and beat until incorporated. Slowly add the beer, beating until a soft, smooth dough forms. You may not need all of the beer.

Position a rack in the lower third of the oven and a rack in the top third of the oven and preheat the oven to 350°F (180°C). Line a large sheet pan with parchment paper.

COOK'S NOTES: The filling can be prepared up to 1 week in advance and stored in an airtight container in the refrigerator. When shaping the empanadas, you will have more filling than you need. You can use leftover filling as a shortcut to make Chipotle Mashed Sweet Potatoes (page 235).

To freeze the empanadas, fill and shape them as directed, then arrange them on the sheet pan and place in the freezer until frozen solid. Transfer them to an airtight container and freeze for up to 3 months. When you're ready to bake them, simply pop them out of the freezer onto a lined sheet pan, brush with the egg wash, puncture with fork tines, and bake as directed, adding a few minutes to the overall time. You can also freeze the baked empanadas if you like, though the flaky texture of the crust will suffer in cold storage.

Turn the dough out onto a lightly floured work surface and bring it together with your hands. Divide the dough into 14 equal pieces and shape each piece into a ball. Cover the balls with a kitchen towel to prevent them from drying out. Working in small batches, on the floured surface, flatten each dough ball slightly, then roll out into a thin round about 4 inches (10 cm) in diameter. Place a small dollop (about 2 tablespoons) of filling on half each dough round. Using a pastry brush, dampen the edge of the round with the egg wash and fold the uncovered side over the filling to create a half-moon. Press the edges together with you fingers and then with the tines of a fork to seal securely. Repeat until all the dough rounds are filled.

Brush the top of each empanada with the egg wash, then puncture the top twice with fork tines to allow steam to escape during baking. Arrange the empanadas on the prepared sheet pan, spacing them about 1 inch (2.5 cm) apart. Place the pan on the lowest oven rack and bake the empanadas until lightly golden, about 25 minutes. If after 15 minutes the bottoms of the empanadas are starting to brown, move the sheet pan to the top rack.

Set the oven to broil, move the pan to the top rack (if it is not already there), and broil until the tops are golden brown, 1–2 minutes. Transfer the empanadas to wire racks to cool. Serve warm or at room temperature.

MEXICAN
Sangria

The flavor of this sangria reminds me of the sangria served in a restaurant in Ciudad Juárez, Mexico, called Chihuahua Charlie's. The restaurant no longer exists, but its sangria infused with *canela* (cinnamon) and chopped fresh fruits remains a vivid memory—and a beverage that I crave. A glass of red wine is a must with Thanksgiving dinner. What I love about this sangria is that it goes further than wine. It is super flavorful, and when served in a clear-glass pitcher, it displays a bounty of fruits that lends a beautiful festive touch.

MAKES 12 SERVINGS

1 orange, sliced

1 apple, cored and chopped

1 pear, cored and chopped

1 cinnamon stick

4 whole cloves

1 cup (240 ml) Cointreau

2 bottles (750 ml each) red wine, preferably Tempranillo

1 bottle (1 l) club soda, chilled

Ice cubes (optional)

Drop the orange, apple, pear, cinnamon stick, and cloves into a clear-glass pitcher and pour in the Cointreau and wine. Stir well, cover, and refrigerate overnight.

Just before serving, stir in the club soda. Serve chilled, over ice if desired.

TORTA & TACO BAR
with Thanksgiving leftovers

Tortas (sandwiches) are a convenient and tasty national tradition that Mexicans enjoy anytime of the day and evening. My mom always made tortas for our family car trips, and I have made countless tortas for my children's school lunches. Hosting a torta and taco bar is a great way to finish off your Thanksgiving leftovers. Set out the items listed below with whatever else you like, such as cheese, avocado, tomato, onion, lettuce, and limes and invite your guests to make their own tortas and tacos.

— ❧⚬❧ —

Shredded or sliced turkey (page 240)

Bolillos, homemade (page 232) or store-bought

Salsas of your choice

Rajas con Queso (page 236)

Tortillas (corn and fried shells)

CHRISTMAS,
NEW YEAR'S EVE,
and Epiphany

Unlike in the United States where Christmas celebrations are mainly limited to Christmas Eve and Christmas Day, Mexican celebrations span nearly an entire month. So what does that mean? That means lots of opportunities for fiestas, of course! In this chapter, I share both classic and modern Mexican Christmas drinks and dishes that will liven up your holiday menus.

Mexican Christmas celebrations officially start with the feast day for our patron saint, Our Lady of Guadalupe (Día de la Virgen de Guadalupe), on December 12. A mainstay of that day's festivities are *buñuelos*, crisp, golden fritters topped with a sticky-sweet *piloncillo* syrup.

From December 16 until Christmas Eve, December 24, a tradition known as *Las Posadas* is celebrated. *Posada* is the Spanish word for "inn" or "lodging," and each evening during this period, families and neighbors dress up and walk through the streets in a reenactment of the difficult journey made by Mary and Joseph from Nazareth to Bethlehem in search of a warm place to stay for the night and where their son, Jesus, could be born. To keep everyone nice and warm despite the chilly winter air, cups of spicy Mexican Hot Chocolate and sweetly caffeinated *café de olla* (page 67) are passed out to the throngs of walkers.

On *Nochebuena* (Christmas Eve), it is traditional to attend Midnight Mass. When I was growing up, our family always went to Midnight Mass, but once I had my own family, my celebration moved to Mass on Christmas Day morning and a big dinner later in the day. Colorful Ensalada de Nochebuena and Turkey Pozole Verde make delicious dishes for the dining table.

In some states in Mexico, children expect Santa Claus on December 24, while in southern Mexico, children await their presents on January 6, Epiphany, which is known as *El Día de los Reyes*. Before Santa arrives, we like to set out a glass of milk and a platter of *biscochos* and *polvorones* to keep him and the reindeer well-fed for their journey.

While the kids gleefully open their presents, my hubby and I love to sip spiked *café de olla*.

ENSALADA
de Nochebuena

Christmas Eve is a time for family and friends to gather and eat, drink, and be merry. This traditional and colorful salad is loaded with crunchy romaine, pepitas, apples and earthy beets, tart citrus, prickly pear, and pomegranate, all dressed with a sweet, creamy dressing. It is a welcome departure from the rich fare that dominates the rest of the holiday table.

MAKES 4–6 SERVINGS

DRESSING

½ cup (100 g) plain Greek yogurt

3 tablespoons pomegranate juice (from the pomegranate garnish)

1½ tablespoons honey

1 teaspoon grated orange zest

SALAD

2 cups (150 g) chopped romaine lettuce

2 medium beets, cooked, peeled, and thinly sliced

2 oranges or mandarins, peeled and segmented

½ cup (60 g) matchstick-cut, peeled jicama

1 apple, halved, cored, and sliced

1 prickly pear or kiwi, peeled and sliced

GARNISH

½ cup (90 g) pomegranate seeds (from about 1 pomegranate; reserve juice for the dressing)

¼ cup (35 g) Spicy Roasted Pepitas (page 191)

To make the dressing, whisk together the yogurt, pomegranate juice, honey, and orange zest, mixing well.

To assemble the salad, make a bed of the lettuce on a large platter. Arrange the beets, oranges, jicama, apple, and prickly pear on top of the lettuce in concentric circles.

Drizzle the dressing over the salad. Garnish with the pomegranate seeds and pepitas and serve.

TURKEY *Pozole Verde*

Pozole is a simple, rustic soup made from hominy and can be white, red, or green. In this green version, the flavorful broth is made with a *salsa verde* that includes tomatillos, cilantro, and jalapeños, which gives the soup its beautiful green hue, and toasted pumpkin seeds, which contribute a nutty flavor and creamy texture. This recipe is good to have on hand during the Christmas and New Year's holidays when you typically have turkey leftovers on hand and a hearty meal is always welcome.

———— ⋯•⋯ ————

MAKES 8–12 SERVINGS

SALSA VERDE

1½ lb (680 g) tomatillos, husked and rinsed

½ cup (80 g) chopped white onion

1–2 jalapeño chiles, stemmed

3 cloves garlic, smashed and peeled

Handful of fresh cilantro leaves

¼ cup (35 g) raw pepitas (hull-free pumpkin seeds), toasted

1 teaspoon kosher salt

SOUP

4 cups (950 ml) chicken broth

2½ cups (600 ml) water

1 small white onion, quartered

2 cloves garlic, coarsely chopped

1 teaspoon kosher salt

3 cups (450 g) shredded cooked turkey (page 240)

2 cans (29 oz/825 g each) Mexican-style hominy, drained

Jalapeño slices, diced white onion, radish slices, chopped fresh cilantro, dried Mexican oregano, and lime wedges, for garnish

Tostadas, for serving

To make the salsa verde, in a large saucepan, combine the tomatillos, onion, jalapeños, garlic, and water to cover generously. Bring to a boil over medium-high heat and boil until the tomatillos turn light green, about 8 minutes. Drain well in a colander, discarding the liquid.

Transfer the boiled tomatillos, onion, jalapeños, and garlic to a blender, add the cilantro, pepitas, and salt, and blend until smooth. Transfer to a bowl and set aside. Rinse out the blender.

To make the soup, in a 6-quart (5.7-l) pot over high heat, combine the broth, water, onion, garlic, and salt and bring to a boil. Reduce the heat to medium-low and simmer gently for 10 minutes.

Transfer 1 cup (240 ml) of the broth to the blender along with the onion and garlic and blend until smooth. Return the blended mixture to the broth remaining in the pot. Add the salsa verde, turkey, and hominy, cover partially, and bring everything to a boil over medium-high heat. Reduce the heat to medium-low and simmer gently for 20 minutes to blend the flavors. While the pozole is simmering, set out all the garnishes in bowls or on plates on the table.

When the pozole is ready, taste and adjust the seasoning with salt if needed. Then ladle the pozole into soup bowls and serve with tostadas. Invite your guests to add garnishes as they like.

 COOK'S NOTE: No turkey leftovers? Poach 2 lb (1 kg) boneless, skinless chicken breasts, let cool, and then shred.

ORANGE
Biscochos

Biscochos are popular Christmas cookies in El Paso. In New Mexico, they are known as both *bizcochitos* and Native American Pueblo Feast Day cookies. In Mexico, they are called *hojarascas* or *pan de polvo. Hojarascas* is Spanish for "fallen leaves," and the cookies are so named because the crunch of stepping on dry leaves is thought to be similar to the sound you hear when you take a bite of a shortbread-like *biscocho.*

These cookies are usually made in large batches for weddings and other special occasions and are traditionally flavored with aniseeds. This recipe is similar to the recipe my mom has made for years but without the aniseeds and with butter-flavored shortening in place of lard. The dough is flavored with orange juice, orange liqueur, and orange zest, and I have also added orange zest to the coating of cinnamon sugar. Although these cookies are delicate and crumbly, they do not fall apart too easily, and they are totally addicting.

ABOUT 100 SMALL COOKIES

3 cups (375 g) all-purpose flour

1 teaspoon baking powder

½ teaspoon salt

1 tablespoon ground cinnamon, preferably freshly ground

⅛ teaspoon ground ginger

¼ cup (60 ml) fresh orange juice

2 tablespoons orange liqueur

1 teaspoon pure vanilla extract

1 tablespoon grated orange zest

1 cup (225 g) butter-flavored solid vegetable shortening

¾ cup (150 g) sugar

1 large egg

Preheat the oven to 350°F (180°C). Have ready 2 sheet pans.

In a medium bowl, whisk together the flour, baking powder, salt, cinnamon, and ginger, mixing well. In a small bowl, stir together the orange juice, orange liqueur, vanilla, and orange zest, mixing well.

In a stand mixer fitted with the paddle attachment, beat the shortening on medium speed until creamy. Add the sugar and egg and beat until smooth. On low speed, add the flour mixture in three batches alternately with the orange juice mixture in two batches, beginning and ending with the flour mixture and beating after each addition just until incorporated. Remove the bowl from the mixer stand and lightly knead the dough with your hands to bring it together.

Remove some dough from the bowl (the amount will vary depending on the size of your cookie press) and cover the bowl with a damp kitchen towel to prevent the remaining dough from drying out. Shape the dough into a log that fits your cookie press, then slip the log into your press. Holding the press upright and resting it on a sheet pan, apply even pressure to the handle to release a cookie. Move the press and repeat, spacing the cookies about 1 inch (2.5 cm) apart, until the sheet pan is full.

CINNAMON SUGAR

½ cup (100 g) sugar

¼ teaspoon ground cinnamon, preferably freshly ground

1 teaspoon grated orange zest

COOK'S NOTES: You can also roll out this dough about ¼ inch (6 mm) thick and cut out the cookies with a cookie cutter. But I like to use a cookie press because I can make smaller cookies and shape them more quickly. If the dough is dry or feels too "thick" to pass through your cookie press, add a little more orange juice to it as needed to ease it through the press.

The recipe makes lots of cookies, and they freeze beautifully. Pull out a few from the freezer when you have company or give them as melt-in-your-mouth Christmas gifts.

Bake the cookies until they are lightly browned around the edges, 8–10 minutes.

While the cookies are baking, make the cinnamon sugar. On a plate, mix together the sugar, cinnamon, and orange zest. Then ready another batch of cookies for the oven.

When the cookies are ready, remove from the oven and slide the second batch into the oven. Transfer the just-baked cookies to a wire rack to cool slightly, then roll them in the cinnamon sugar, coating on all sides, and return them to the rack to cool completely. Shape, bake, and coat the remaining cookies the same way, always making sure the sheet pan has cooled before adding a new batch.

The cookies will keep in resealable plastic bags in the refrigerator for up to 1 week or in the freezer for up to 6 months.

RED, WHITE & GREEN
Polvorones

A popular offering in Mexican *panaderías* (bakeries), these tricolor shortbread cookies, which are known as *polvorones*, *payasos*, or *galletas*, are tender and lightly crunchy. They are traditionally pink, chocolate, and yellow, but I have made them red, white, and green for Christmas. The dough is the same dough I use for the Mexican Sprinkle Cookies on page 84.

MAKES 21–23 COOKIES

1 cup (225 g) butter-flavored solid vegetable shortening, plus more for the pan

1 cup (200 g) sugar

1 large egg

2 teaspoons pure vanilla extract

2 cups (250 g) all-purpose flour, plus more for dusting

⅛ teaspoon salt

Red food coloring

Green food coloring

In a bowl, using an electric mixer, beat the shortening on medium speed until light and fluffy. Add the sugar and salt and continue to beat on medium speed until smooth, about 1 minute. On low speed, add the egg and vanilla and beat until well combined, 2–3 minutes.

Turn off the mixer, add about one-third of the flour, and then turn the mixer on low and beat until the flour is incorporated. Repeat with the remaining flour, adding one-third of the flour each time and always turning off the mixture before each addition.

When all the flour has been incorporated, turn the dough out onto a lightly floured work surface and divide the dough into 3 equal portions (about 8½ oz/240 g each). Put 2 portions in separate glass bowls. Leave the third portion on the work surface.

Add a small amount of the red food coloring to the dough in 1 bowl, working it into the dough to color it evenly and adding more coloring if needed to get the color you want. Repeat with green food coloring and the dough in the second bowl.

On a lightly floured work surface, roll the red, green, and white doughs into 3 separate logs each 10 inches (25 cm) long. Place 2 logs side by side and place the third log in the center on top. Roll gently to fuse the trio of colors together, shaping the logs into a triangular prism.

Preheat the oven to 350°F (180°C). Grease a sheet pan with shortening.

Spread flour on a small plate. Dip the edge of a bench scraper or a sharp knife into the flour, then then cut the dough into cookies ¼ inch (6 mm) thick, dipping the scraper into the flour before each cut. Arrange the cookies on the prepared sheet pan, spacing them 2 inches (5 cm) apart.

Bake the cookies until the bottoms are lightly golden, 12–14 minutes. Transfer to a wire rack and let cool completely before serving. Store leftover cookies in an airtight container at room temperature for up to 5 days.

COOK'S NOTE: The same dough can be used to make many different polvorones, depending on the celebration. The only thing you will change is the shape and the food coloring. Roll out the dough ¼ inch (6 mm) thick. For Valentine's Day, use red or pink food coloring and a heart-shaped cookie cutter; for Saint Patrick's Day, use green food coloring and a four-leaf-clover cookie cutter; for Halloween, use orange food coloring and a pumpkin-shaped cutter; and for Easter, use a pastel food coloring and a flower-shaped cutter. The possibilities are many!

BUÑUELOS
with Gingerbread Piloncillo Syrup

Buñuelos are made by rolling out dough into thin rounds (much like a flour tortilla), deep-frying them, and then coating them with cinnamon sugar. They are a classic crispy and sweet Mexican Christmas dessert with traditional American Christmas flavors. You can make a simpler piloncillo syrup similar to the one in my French toast recipe (page 117), but this one is more festive, making it perfect for Christmastime. The syrup is also good drizzled on pancakes and used in coffee and cocktails, and it makes a nice edible holiday gift.

MAKES 16 BUÑUELOS

PILONCILLO SYRUP

1 cup (240 ml) water

½ lb (225 g) piloncillo, chopped, or 1 cup (210 g) packed dark brown sugar

1 cinnamon stick

4 whole cloves

½ teaspoon ground ginger

½ teaspoon ground allspice

¼ teaspoon black peppercorns

1 tablespoon honey

BUÑUELOS

3 cups (375 g) all-purpose flour, plus more for dusting

1 teaspoon baking powder

1 teaspoon salt

1 teaspoon ground cinnamon

¾ cup (180 ml) whole milk

4 tablespoons (60 g) unsalted butter

1 teaspoon pure vanilla extract

2 large eggs, lightly beaten

Canola oil, for deep-frying

To make the syrup, in a heavy saucepan over medium-high heat, combine the water, piloncillo, cinnamon, and cloves and bring to a boil, stirring to dissolve the piloncillo. Reduce the heat to low, add the ginger, allspice, peppercorns, and honey, stir well, and simmer uncovered for 5 minutes until a syrup forms. Remove from the heat, cover, and let steep for 30 minutes. Pour through a fine-mesh sieve and discard the solids in the sieve. Set aside until needed.

To make the buñuelos, in a large bowl, whisk together the flour, baking powder, salt, and cinnamon. In a small saucepan over medium heat, combine the milk, butter, and vanilla and heat just until the butter melts. Remove from the heat and let cool to room temperature. Whisk the eggs into the room-temperature milk mixture, blending well.

Add the milk mixture to the flour mixture and mix until a rough dough forms that comes away from the sides of the bowl. Turn the dough out onto a lightly floured work surface and knead until soft and smooth, 2–3 minutes.

Divide the dough into 16 equal portions and shape each portion into a ball. Lay a tablecloth on a nearby surface to use for the rounds once they are rolled out. On a lightly floured work surface, roll out each ball into a thin round about 8 inches (20 cm) in diameter. As the rounds are ready, transfer them to the tablecloth.

When all the rounds are on the tablecloth, let them dry, turning them over once, for about 30 minutes. This helps remove most of the moisture before frying, resulting in a crispier buñuelo that absorbs less oil while cooking. Prick each round once with fork times to prevent bubbles from forming during frying.

CINNAMON SUGAR

1 cup (200 g) sugar

1 teaspoon ground cinnamon

COOK'S NOTES: Buñuelos will keep their crunch and texture for up to 3 days. I recommend stacking them on a plate, covering them lightly with a paper towel, and storing them at room temperature.

The piloncillo syrup will keep in an airtight container in the refrigerator for up to 2 weeks. Bring to room temperature before serving.

To make the cinnamon sugar, in a small bowl, stir together the sugar and cinnamon, mixing well.

Select a bowl large enough to hold the dough rounds vertically once they are fried, line it with paper towels, and set it near the stove. Select a frying pan large enough to hold a dough round flat. Pour the oil to a depth of 1 inch (2.5 cm) into the pan and heat over medium-high heat to 350°F (180°C) on a deep-frying thermometer. Add a dough round to the hot oil and fry, turning once, until golden brown on both sides, 1–2 minutes on each side. As it cooks, press gently with tongs if needed to prevent curling. Using tongs, transfer the buñuelo to the towel-lined bowl, standing it upright, to drain. Repeat with the remaining dough rounds, sprinkling them on both sides with the cinnamon sugar while they are still warm.

Serve the buñuelos warm, drizzled with the piloncillo syrup.

ROSCA *de Navidad*

This marbled and twirly-topped bread is a cross between a Christmas star and a *rosca de reyes*, or "king's cake," a wreath-shaped cake that is traditionally baked for Día de los Reyes in Mexico. The bread is decorated with candied fruits to symbolize the "jewels" on a crown and has a small plastic or ceramic figure tucked inside to represent the baby Jesus. Known as Epiphany in other parts of the world, Día de los Reyes falls on January 6 and celebrates the visit the Three Wise Men made to Bethlehem to bring gifts to the baby Jesus. The custom is that whoever finds the figurine in his or her serving of the bread must host a party on Día de la Candelaria (Candlemas Day), a Christian festival day celebrated on February 2 at which tamales are traditionally served.

MAKES 9 SERVINGS

1 package (2¼ teaspoons) active dry yeast

¼ cup (60 ml) warm water (110°–115°F/43°–46°C)

¾ cup warm milk (110°–115°F/43°–46°C)

½ teaspoon pure vanilla extract

½ teaspoon pure lemon extract

1 large egg, at room temperature

4 tablespoons (60 g) unsalted butter, at room temperature, plus more for the bowl and pan and 2 tablespoons, melted, for finishing

¼ cup (50 g) sugar

1 teaspoon salt

3¼–3¾ cups (405–470 g) all-purpose flour

¾ cup (240 g) seedless raspberry jam

1 small figurine (optional)

Candied lemon peel and maraschino cherries, for garnish

In a small bowl, dissolve the yeast in the warm water and let stand until foamy, about 5 minutes. In the bowl of a stand mixer fitted with the paddle attachment, beat together the milk, vanilla and lemon extracts, egg, room-temperature butter, sugar, and salt on low speed until incorporated. Add the yeast mixture and 3 cups (375 g) of the flour and beat on medium speed until smooth, about 1 minute. Remove the bowl from the mixer stand and stir in enough of the remaining flour to form a soft dough.

Turn the dough out onto a lightly floured surface and knead until smooth and elastic, 6–8 minutes. Shape the dough into a ball. Butter a large bowl, add the dough, and then turn the dough to coat the entire surface with butter. Cover the bowl with a kitchen towel and let the dough rise in a warm place until doubled in size, about 1 hour.

Line a large baking sheet with parchment paper. Punch down the dough, turn it out onto a lightly floured work surface, and divide it into 4 equal portions. Cover 3 portions with a kitchen towel. Roll out the remaining portion into a round 12 inches (30 cm) in diameter. Transfer the round to the prepared baking sheet. Spread one-third of the jam over the round, leaving a ½-inch (12-mm) border uncovered. Repeat twice, layering a dough round with one-third of the jam each time, and then finish with a dough round.

Place a 2½-inch (6-cm) round cutter in the center of the top dough round (do not press down). Using a sharp knife, make 18 evenly spaced cuts from the edge of the round cutter to the edge of dough, cutting through all 4 layers of the dough and forming a starburst.

Remove the cutter. Grasp 2 adjacent strips, rotate them twice outward, and pinch the ends together. Repeat with the remaining strips. Cover with a kitchen towel and let rise until almost doubled in size, about 30 minutes. About 20 minutes before the rise is over, preheat the oven to 375°F (190°C).

Bake the bread until golden brown, about 20 minutes. Remove from the oven and immediately brush with the melted butter, avoiding areas where jam is visible. Transfer to a wire rack and let cool completely.

If using, tuck the figurine into one of the slits of the bread. Decorate with candied lemon peel and maraschino cherries. Serve warm or at room temperature.

POINSETTIA
Punch

A riff on the Champagne cocktail, this rose-tinted sparkling wine punch is flavored with orange and cranberry. The addition of floating frozen orange slices and cranberries to the bowl keeps the punch well chilled and looking beautiful.

MAKES 24 SERVINGS

2 oranges, thinly sliced

⅔ cup (70 g) fresh cranberries

3 cups (700 ml) cranberry juice, chilled

¾ cup (180 ml) orange liqueur, chilled

2 bottles (750 ml each) brut sparkling wine, cava, or Champagne, chilled

Arrange the orange slices and cranberries in a single layer on a sheet pan or dish and freeze until solid, about 1 hour.

When ready to serve, pour the cranberry juice and liqueur into a punch bowl and stir to mix well. Then pour in the sparkling wine. Float the frozen orange slices and cranberries in the punch and serve immediately.

 COOK'S NOTES: To keep the punch cool, chill the punch bowl in the freezer or refrigerator before filling it.

To make an ice ring for the punch bowl, put the cranberries and orange slices in a Bundt pan or other tube pan and add just enough cranberry juice to cover the fruit. Freeze for 8 hours. Unmold the ice ring from the pan and add it to the filled punch bowl.

TAMALADA

A *tamalada* is a traditional Mexican party at which family and friends get together to make tamales. Homemade tamales are delicious year-round, but it is customary to make a big batch around the Christmas holidays. They freeze well, so don't be shy!

Making tamales is labor-intensive, but the process itself isn't difficult. By hosting a *tamalada*, you are certain to crank out more tamales than you could possibly make alone, and at the end, everyone takes home tamales and wonderful memories.
Think of a *tamalada* as a sewing circle with food! It is one of my favorite things to do every winter. And when you have the help of many hands, you can more easily make lots of different types of tamales.

If you have little ones who want to get in on the action, set up a crafting table for them to make mini tamal-shaped ornaments (see page 278). There's no sewing or hot glue involved, so you won't need to keep too close a watch. Plus, they'll get lots of practice for when they're old enough to help in the kitchen!

How to Host a Tamalada

First, to make hosting less stressful, assign a few guests to bring filling options and/or an appetizer to share, and you take care of making the masa (dough), soaking the corn husks, and all the beverages.

Tamal Fillings

The possible fillings for tamales are many. Traditional red chile and chicken and shredded barbacoa (page 73) are two favorites of mine. Jalapeño and cheese is an easy vegetarian filling that can be made with homemade (page 161) or store-bought pickled jalapeños, and sweet raisin just like my grandma used to make is ideal for kid-friendly dessert tamales.

Teach the Art of Tamal-Making

Demonstrate how to make the first tamal and then have your guests roll up their sleeves and take part in the filling and wrapping.

Steam the Tamales

Set up and fill the steamer with the tamales. Then, as the little bundles steam and fill the house with fantastic aromas, invite everyone to snack on appetizers and sip Poinsettia Punch (page 265) or Mexican Hot Chocolate (page 277).

Enjoy

Once the tamales are cooked, it is time to feast. Freshly steamed tamales are fun to open and eat, making them the perfect party food. A *tamalada* is as much about cooking together as it is about eating together.

Send Guests Home with Tamales

The average recipe makes dozens of tamales, so plan on sharing leftovers. I purchase large resealable plastic bags and send guests home with a dozen tamales.

RED CHILE & CHICKEN
Tamales

MAKES ABOUT 30 TAMALES

FILLING

4 lb (1.8 kg) boneless, skinless chicken breasts

1¼ cups (300 ml) water

1½ teaspoons sea salt

1 clove garlic

1 white onion, quartered

3 tablespoons chicken broth

1½ teaspoons all-purpose flour

3½ cups (825 ml) Red Chile Sauce (page 17)

MASA

1 lb (450 g) lard, plus more if needed

1 tablespoon salt

1 teaspoon baking powder

2½ lb (1.1 kg) fresh masa (unprepared) for tamales

1–1½ cups (240–350 ml) broth from cooked chicken

¼ cup (60 ml) Red Chile Sauce (page 17), optional

Corn husks (hojas)

To make the filling, in a large stockpot over medium-high heat, combine the chicken, water, salt, garlic, and onion and bring to a boil. Adjust the heat to a simmer and simmer uncovered until cooked through, about 25 minutes. Remove from the heat. Transfer the chicken to a platter, let cool, and then shred and set aside.

Transfer the contents of the pot to a blender and blend until smooth. This flavorful mixture can be used as part of the broth for the filling and for the masa. It will keep in an airtight container in the refrigerator for up to 1 week or in the freezer for up to 4 months.

In a large frying pan over medium heat, whisk together the broth and flour until the mixture is lump-free, 4–5 minutes. Slowly add the chile sauce, stirring constantly to avoid lumps, and then cook, stirring occasionally, for 10 minutes. At the end of this time, the chile sauce will be very thick.

Add the shredded chicken and stir until all the chicken is well coated with the chile sauce. Simmer for about 10 minutes to blend the flavors. Remove from the heat and let cool before using.

To make the masa, in a stand mixer fitted with the paddle attachment, beat the lard on medium speed until fluffy, stopping to scrape down the sides of the bowl as needed to keep the lard in the center of the bowl. Add the salt and baking powder and beat until incorporated. On medium-low speed, add the masa and beat until well mixed. With the mixer still on medium-low speed, slowly add 1 cup (240 ml) broth and the chile sauce, if using, and mix until smooth. The mixture should be about the consistency of creamy peanut butter. If it isn't, add more broth as needed to achieve a good consistency. To test if the masa is ready, drop a small piece (about ½ teaspoon) into a small bowl of warm water. If it floats, it is ready; if it sinks, add a little more lard, beat for another minute, and test it again. Remove the bowl from the mixer stand, cover with a kitchen towel, and set the masa aside while the corn husks soak.

Continues on the following page

El que nace para tamal,
del cielo le caen las hojas

Continued from the previous page

COOK'S NOTES: You can cook the chicken in an Instant Pot. Secure the lid in place and pressure cook on high for 15 minutes. Let the steam release naturally for 5 minutes, then do a quick release.

Put a penny or two on the bottom of the pot used for steaming before you add the water, then steam as directed. When you hear the penny rattle, it means the water level is low and it is time to add more water to the pot.

ADDITIONAL TAMAL FILLINGS

Barbacoa de Borrego (page 73)

Lamb Birria (page 99)

Chile Braised Short Ribs (page 211)

Chiles en Escabeche (page 161) with a slice of

Monterey jack or Oaxaca cheese

Pipián Verde (page 61) mixed with shredded chicken

Rajas con Queso (page 236)

Always soak more corn husks than the number of tamales you are making, as some may be too thick, too narrow, or tear, and you will need to tear some into strips for tying the tamales. Rinse the corn husks well to remove any dust and loose fibers, then soak them in water to cover for 1 hour. To keep the husks pliable and easy to work with, leave them in the water while filling the tamales, transferring just a handful at a time to a colander to drain well before using. A strip of husk is used to tie each tamal, so ready some strips—just pull narrow strips lengthwise from a soaked husk—before you begin assembling the tamales.

To assemble each tamal, lay a corn husk on your nondominant hand with the wide end on your palm and the narrow end extending beyond your fingers. Starting at the middle of the husk, and using the back or a spoon, spread about 2 tablespoons of the masa in a rectangular or oval shape, using a downward motion toward the wide bottom end, stopping just short of the edge, and leaving a roughly 2-inch (5-cm) border uncovered on the left and right sides of the husk.

Spoon about 1½ tablespoons of the filling down the center of the masa. Fold the uncovered sides of the husk to the center, then fold the narrow end of the husk over the filled end. Make sure it is a snug closure so the tamal will not open during steaming. Secure the tamal by tying a corn husk strip around it. This will keep the tamal from unwrapping during the steaming process, especially if the husk is a bit thick and resists folding. Repeat to make the remaining tamales.

INSTANT POT VARIATION: Pour 1 cup (240 ml) water into a 6-quart (5.7-l) Instant Pot and insert the steam rack.

Arrange a few soaked corn husks on the bottom of the rack. Arrange 12 tamales, vertically and open end up, on the corn husks. Lock the lid in place, select the manual setting, and cook on high pressure for 38 minutes. Let the steam release naturally for about 10 minutes, then do a quick release to release any residual steam. Carefully remove the lid and transfer the tamales to a plate. Let stand for 15–30 minutes to set up before serving.

Use a tamalera (specially designed pot for steaming tamales) or a large, deep pot with a tight-fitting lid and a perforated rack to steam the tamales. If using a tamalera, fill it with water to the fill line and set the rack over the water. If using a deep pot, add water to a depth of about 3 inches (7.5 cm), then prop the steamer rack above the water. Arrange the tamales vertically, open side up and folded sides against one another (to keep them from unfolding), on the rack. Cover the pot tightly, turn on the heat to high, and bring the water to a boil, about 15 minutes. Reduce the heat to a simmer and steam for 2½–3 hours. Always keep the pot tightly covered unless you need to add water to it. To test if the tamales are ready, transfer a tamal to a plate, let sit for a couple of minutes, and then open it. If the husk lifts away without sticking to the tamal, they are done.

Let the tamales sit for 5–10 minutes before serving.

SWEET RAISIN
Tamales

MAKE 24–30 TAMALES

PILONCILLO SYRUP

1–1½ cups (240–350 ml) water

1 cinnamon stick

5 whole cloves

½ lb (225 g) piloncillo, chopped, or 1 cup (210 g) packed dark brown sugar

MASA

1 lb (450 g) lard

½ teaspoon baking powder

½ teaspoon salt

2 teaspoons vanilla exract

2½ lb (1.1 kg) fresh masa (unprepared) for tamales

1 cup (240 ml) piloncillo syrup, at room temperature (above)

1¼ cups (200 g) raisins, soaked in water for 30 minutes, then drained

Corn husks (hojas)

To make the syrup, in a small, heavy saucepan over high heat, combine the water (use less water for sweeter tamales), cinnamon, and cloves and bring to a boil. Remove from the heat, cover, and let steep for 30 minutes. Remove and discard the cinnamon and cloves.

Return the pan to low heat, add the piloncillo, and heat, stirring occasionally, until the piloncillo dissolves and a thin syrup forms, about 15 minutes. Remove from the heat and let cool. You will need only 1 cup (240 ml) of the syrup for the masa. The remainder will keep in an airtight container for up to 2 weeks. Use for drizzling on buñuelos (page 260) or Caballeros Pobres (page 117).

To make the masa, in a stand mixer fitted with the paddle attachment, beat the lard on medium speed until fluffy, stopping to scrape down the sides of the bowl as needed to keep the lard in the center of the bowl. Add the baking powder and salt and beat until incorporated. On medium-low speed, add fresh masa and beat until well mixed. With the mixer still on medium-low speed, slowly add the piloncillo syrup and raisins and beat just until evenly blended. Remove the bowl from the mixer stand, cover with a kitchen towel, and set the masa aside while the corn husks soak.

Always soak more corn husks than the number of tamales you are making, as some may be too thick, too narrow, or tear, and you will need to tear some into strips for tying the tamales. Rinse the corn husks well to remove any dust and loose fibers, then soak them in water to cover for 1 hour. To keep the husks pliable and easy to work with, leave them in hot water while filling the tamales, transferring just a handful at a time to a colander to drain well before using. A strip of husk is used to tie each tamal, so ready some strips—just pull narrow strips lengthwise from a soaked husk—before you begin assembling the tamales.

For sweet tamales, I like to simply wrap the husk around the masa, as pictured, and tie the top with a corn husk strip. Scoop about ⅓ cup of the masa onto the center of a corner husk, fold in the sides, and then bring the ends together and tie securely with a husk strip. Repeat to make the remaining tamales.

Use a tamalera (specially designed pot for steaming tamales) or a large, deep pot with a tight-fitting lid and a perforated rack to steam the tamales. If using a tamalera, fill it with water to the fill line and set the rack over the water. If using a deep pot, add water to a depth of about 3 inches (7.5 cm), then prop the steamer rack above the water. Arrange the tamales vertically, tied end up, on the rack. Cover the pot tightly, turn on the heat to high, and bring the water to a boil, about 15 minutes. Reduce the heat to a simmer and steam for 1–1½ hours. Always keep the pot tightly covered unless you need to add water to it. To test if the tamales are ready, transfer a tamal to a plate, let sit for a couple of minutes, and then open it. If the husk lifts away without sticking to the tamal, they are done.

Let the tamales sit for 3–5 minutes before serving.

MEXICAN
Hot Chocolate

My daughter loves Mexican hot chocolate! I used to make it every Christmas and now that she is older she loves to make it for every fall and winter special occasion. Serve this warm chocolate for Día de los Muertos, *tamaladas*, or Christmas morning.

MAKES 8 SERVINGS

8 cups (1.9 l) water, plus ¼ cup (60 ml)

3 cinnamon sticks

6 oz (170 g) Mexican chocolate, broken into pieces

¼ cup (30 g) cornstarch

1 cup (240 ml) whole milk or almond or other dairy-free milk

Kahlúa or peppermint schnapps, for serving (optional)

In a saucepan over high heat, combine the 8 cups (1.9 l) water and cinnamon and bring to a boil. Remove from the heat, cover, and let steep for 1 hour. Remove and discard the cinnamon.

Return the pan with the water to medium-low heat, add the chocolate, and stir until melted. While the chocolate is melting, in a small bowl, dissolve the cornstarch in the remaining ¼ cup (60 ml) water, stirring well to prevent lumps. Once the chocolate is melted, slowly add the cornstarch slurry while stirring constantly.

Pour in the milk and let the mixture come to a slow boil, stirring often. The moment it boils, remove the pan from the heat and serve at once in mugs. For an adult-spiked hot chocolate, add a splash of Kahlúa to the mug.

COOK'S NOTE: The hot chocolate will thicken a little more and be creamier if made with whole cow's milk rather than a dairy-free milk.

Tamal-Shaped Christmas Ornaments

If you love the idea of crafting but feel too intimidated to start, try making these super-easy tamal-shaped tree ornaments. Kids will like making them too. They are a great way to spread cheer at holiday time, so make enough to hand out to family and friends.

Materials

Corn husks

Fiber filling

Small rubber bands

Ribbon or narrow strips of pretty fabric, for tying

Twine or ribbon, for hanging

Soak the corn husks in water to cover until pliable, about 1 hour. Drain well and pat dry. To assemble each ornament, put a small handful of fiber filling on the center of a husk and wrap the husk around it. Secure the top with a rubber band, then tie the top with ribbon or fabric. I like to cut a colorful fabric swatch into strips for a rustic look. Finally, add a loop of twine or ribbon to use for hanging.

FAMILY
Fiestas

One of the things I love most about my culture is that Mexican American families have a strong foundation of family and community. As enthusiastic and joyful people, we take any opportunity we can to celebrate!

The larger your community, the more family celebrations—quinceañeras, weddings, baby showers, baptisms, first communions, confirmations—you will have throughout the year. That doesn't even account for other reasons to gather, such as birthdays or graduations (or new cookbook releases!).

These celebratory get-togethers are typically a time for serving dishes rooted in tradition, and in this chapter, I am sharing a handful of my favorite time-honored recipes for special occasions.

One of the most rewarding Mexican dishes I have learned to make is mole. My recipe is a little bit grandma and a little bit mom mixed with some techniques I learned while visiting Oaxaca. Mole is not difficult to make from scratch, and I promise you your guests will be impressed.

If you have an occasion to celebrate, it is always a good idea to make a big batch of *polvorones*, or Mexican wedding cookies. These crumbly, buttery cookies are a huge crowd-pleaser, and despite their name, they're not just for weddings! Every fiesta needs delicious side dishes too. Here I have included two classics: Sopa de Letras (Alphabet Soup) is perfect for a baby shower or kid's birthday party, and Arroz Blanco Mexicano, with its bright, sweet pops of carrots and peas, complements any special-occasion table.

And finally, no celebration is complete without a memorable punch. Serve my colorful and fruity Watermelon-Pineapple Tequila Punch in a watermelon "bowl," making it a festive and fun centerpiece for any party.

I hope that your life is filled with many reasons throughout the year to celebrate and smile with your loved ones. *Salud!*

Donde comen dos, comen tres

ARROZ BLANCO
Mexicano

Arroz (rice) is a staple in Mexican kitchens. For this recipe, which is also known as *arroz primavera* (spring rice), the rice is simmered in a flavorful chicken broth with vegetables, making it a great side dish for everything from grilled meats and seafood to stews. If you are expecting a big group, you can easily double the recipe and cook it in a large frying pan. I don't recommend tripling or quadrupling it, however, unless you use a couple of large pans. Rice is one of those very basic dishes that's challenging to cook well, but practice makes perfect.

MAKES 4 SERVINGS

2 tablespoons butter

1 cup (200 g) long-grain white rice

¼ cup (40 g) chopped white onion

1 clove garlic, finely chopped, or ½ teaspoon garlic paste

2 carrots, peeled and chopped

1¾ cups (425 ml) boiling water

1 package (10 oz/285 g) frozen peas

1½ teaspoons chicken bouillon

Salt

In a frying pan over medium heat, melt the butter. Add the rice and cook, stirring, until lightly browned, about 2 minutes. Add the onion and garlic and stir until the onion is translucent, 1–2 minutes. Add the carrots and cook, stirring, for about 1 minute. Add the water and peas, stir well, and then stir in the bouillon. Let the mixture come to a boil, then reduce the heat to low, cover, and simmer until the rice is fluffy and the carrots are tender, 20–25 minutes.

Remove from the heat and let stand, covered, for about 10 minutes. Uncover, fluff the rice with a fork, season with salt, and serve.

COOK'S NOTE: Rice roughly triples in volume when cooked, so plan on about ¼ cup (50 g) raw rice per person. For serving four people, you'll need to start with 1 cup (200 g) rice.

SOPA
de Letras

Oh, how I used to love this alphabet soup as a kid, and now my kids love it too. Although it is a perfect choice for a child's birthday party, it is also a great everyday comfort food—economical, delicious, and easy to make.

MAKES 6–8 SERVINGS

½ white onion, quartered

3 Roma tomatoes, quartered

1 clove garlic, coarsely chopped

2 tablespoons tomato bouillon

½ teaspoon ground black pepper

4 cups (950 ml) water

2 tablespoons olive oil

1 package (7 oz/200 g) alphabet pasta

Salt

In a blender, combine the onion, tomatoes, garlic, bouillon, pepper, and 1 cup (250 ml) of the water and purée until smooth.

In a Dutch oven over medium heat, warm the oil. Add the alphabet pasta and heat, stirring, until lightly toasted, 1–2 minutes. Add the puréed mixture, stir well, and cook, stirring, until the mixture thickens and darkens, about 5 minutes.

Add the remaining 3 cups (700 ml) water, stir well, and bring to a boil, stirring occasionally. Reduce the heat to low, cover, and cook until the pasta is cooked, about 10 minutes or according to package directions.

Season with salt, ladle into bowls, and serve.

 COOK'S NOTE: Replace the alphabet pasta with fideo or vermicelli for sopa de fideo.

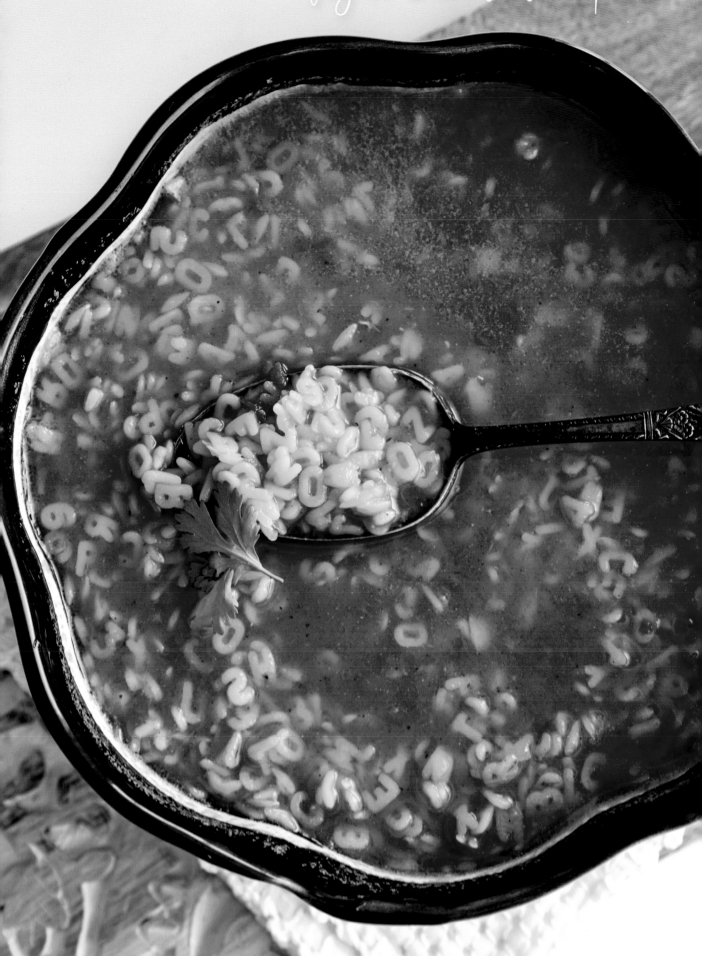

Voy a sacarle la sopa

MOLE ROJO

Nearly every special occasion has a mole on its menu, usually combined with shredded cooked chicken. Mexico boasts scores of different types of traditional moles. Some are sweet from fruit and sugar, some are chile hot, and some are tangy from tomatillos, and they are often defined by color, including *verde* (green; page 61), *negro* (black), *amarillo* (yellow), and *colorado* or *rojo* (red). Although this recipe belongs to the red category, it actually falls between a red mole and a black mole, and it is my favorite—a little bit sweet, a little bit spicy, and a nutty finish! This mole can be drizzled over chicken or simmered with shredded chicken, served as a dipping sauce with tortilla chips, used to make enchiladas or chilaquiles, or simply drizzled over huevos rancheros for a great breakfast.

MAKES 5 CUPS (1.2 L) SAUCE

2 tablespoons olive oil

2 cloves garlic, unpeeled

1 small white onion, quartered

1 bolillo, homemade (page 232) or store-bought, or small French roll, cut into 1-inch (2.5-cm) pieces

2 ancho chiles, stemmed, seeded, and diced

2 dried California or New Mexico red chiles, stemmed, seeded, and diced

2 small tomatillos, husked, rinsed, and chopped

1 tomato, chopped

1 teaspoon sesame seeds, plus more for garnish

1 cinnamon stick

3¾ cups (900 ml) chicken broth

¼ cup (35 g) roasted peanuts

1½ oz (45 g) Mexican chocolate, coarsely chopped

2 teaspoons unsweetened cocoa powder

2 teaspoons salt

In a large frying pan over medium heat, warm the oil. Add the garlic, onion, bolillo, all the chiles, tomatillos, tomato, sesame seeds, and cinnamon and toast, stirring often, for 2 minutes. Remove the garlic from the pan and set aside until cool enough to peel, then peel and reserve. Continue to cook the remaining ingredients, stirring, until they are lightly toasted and soft, about 8 minutes. Transfer to a bowl and set the pan aside to use for the sauce.

Pour half of the broth into a blender and add half of the toasted ingredients. Add the peanuts, chocolate, cocoa powder, and salt and blend until very smooth. Transfer the sauce to the reserved frying pan. Pour the remaining broth into the blender, add the remaining toasted ingredients, blend until very smooth, and add to the pan.

Return the pan to medium heat and bring the sauce to a boil, stirring occasionally. Reduce the heat to low and simmer gently, stirring continuously to prevent sticking to the pan bottom, until thickened and darker in color, 10–15 minutes longer.

Use the sauce right away, garnishing it with sesame seeds, or let cool, transfer to an airtight container, and refrigerate for up to 5 days.

POLVORONES

The name of these buttery, pecan-laced cookies comes from the Spanish word *polvo*, which means "dust" or "powder" and loosely describes their delicious crumbly texture. Also known as Mexican wedding cookies, they make an appearance every Christmas and are also prominently displayed on the main table at weddings, quinceañeras, and other special occasions. Texas is famous for its pecans, so these cookies always taste like home to me. I have also seen them called Russian tea cakes and snowballs, and my late mother-in-law made a similar cookie with chopped almonds, which she called Polish cookies.

MAKES ABOUT 60 COOKIES

2 cups (250 g) all-purpose flour

½ teaspoon salt

1½ cups (170 g) finely chopped pecans

1 cup (225 g) unsalted butter, at room temperature

½ cup (100 g) granulated sugar

2 teaspoons pure vanilla extract

Confectioners' sugar, for dusting

Preheat the oven to 350°F (180°C). Have ready a large sheet pan.

In a medium bowl, whisk together the flour, salt, and pecans. In a large bowl, using an electric mixer, beat together the butter, granulated sugar, and vanilla on medium speed until smooth and creamy. On low speed, gradually add the flour-nut mixture and beat just until well mixed.

To form each cookie, roll 2 teaspoons of the dough between your palms into a ball. Place the balls on the sheet pan, spacing them about ½ inch (12 mm) apart.

Bake the cookies until lightly golden, 15–17 minutes. Transfer to a wire rack and let cool completely.

Gently roll the cooled cookies in confectioners' sugar to coat evenly, then serve. Pack leftover cookies in an airtight container with a little extra confectioners' sugar to keep them well dusted and store at room temperature for up to 10 days.

WATERMELON-PINEAPPLE
Tequila Punch

This refreshing, fruit-based spiked punch can be served in a pitcher or punch bowl,
but if you really want to impress your guests, create a watermelon "bowl."
I top off each glass of punch with a big splash of Topo Chico, naturally carbonated
sparkling water from underground springs near Monterrey, Mexico, that's loaded
with healthy minerals. Although once difficult to find outside Mexico and Texas, it is
now available in stores around the country.

MAKES 12–16 SERVINGS

1 oblong seedless red
watermelon, about 10 lb
(4.5 kg)

2 cups (475 ml) pineapple
juice

2½ cups (600 ml) tequila
blanco

½ cup (120 ml) orange liqueur

½ cup (120 ml) fresh lime
juice (from 4–5 limes)

Ice cubes

Topo Chico, chilled, for
serving

Pineapple wedges, for garnish

Using a long, sharp knife, cut off about one-sixth from the top of
the melon. Then cut a thin slice from the bottom of the melon so
it will sit upright without rocking. Scoop out the flesh into a bowl,
leaving 1 inch (2.5 cm) or so of the flesh at the base. Cover the top
with plastic wrap and set aside in a cool place or in the refrigerator
until serving.

Working in batches, transfer the flesh to a blender and blend until
smooth. Strain through a fine-mesh sieve into a bowl, pressing
against the pulp with the back of a spoon to release as much juice as
possible. Discard the solids in the sieve.

Return the watermelon juice to the blender, add the pineapple juice,
and blend to mix well. Transfer the watermelon-pineapple mixture to
a large pitcher, add the tequila, liqueur, and lime juice, and stir to mix
well. Cover and chill until ready to serve.

To serve, pour the punch into the watermelon bowl. For each serving,
fill a glass with ice, then ladle in the punch, filling the glass three-
fourths full. Top off with a splash of Topo Chico and garnish with a
pineapple wedge.

Acknowledgments

This cookbook is a love letter to my hometown of El Paso, Texas: the art, the food, the people—all of it! I am proud of the border and of the fact that I grew up surrounded by two worlds, Mexico and the United States.

My Muy Bueno readers, fans, and followers: This book is for you. Seeing my recipes made in your *cocina* is what my blog and this book are all about and brings me so much joy. Thank you for all your support and for sharing your stories, reposts, tags, and photos.

My hubby, Bill: Thank you for your unconditional love, patience, constant support, and belief in me.

My mother, Vangie: Thank you for a love so powerful. You are a true superhero! You are my foundation, my rock. You're always there to cheer me on. You helped me develop and test many of the recipes in this book and then helped me cook many of the dishes again when it came time to photograph them. I couldn't have done it without you. You and my grandma Jesusita taught me how to cook through your nurturing and generosity. From you I learned to express my love to my family, friends, and followers with food.

My daughter, Maya, and my son, Blake: You two are my inspiration! Thank you, Maya, for assisting with cooking and styling. I want this book to be a constant reminder of who we are. We are Latinos, loud and proud. May this book share my passion for food and the stories behind it and inspire you both to keep our family traditions alive and to celebrate every occasion *con mucho sabor y amor*.

Dianne Jacob: Thank you for coaching me on my cookbook proposal.

My literary agent, Sally Ekus and the Ekus Group: Thank you for realizing from the beginning that my recipes and crafts deserved a book deal.

Weldon Owen: Thank you for believing in me and my idea for this book. Thank you to the editorial team for your laser eyes and attention to detail. These recipes are concise because of you. Thank you for bringing this book to life and making my book dreams come true.

Ashley Quackenbush and Rita Sowins: Thank you for the beautiful design.

Jenna Sparks: You made my vision come to life with your extraordinary talent as a photographer and your invaluable assistance with food styling. I am truly blessed to have you on my team. Your photographs bring light, love, and passion to every page.

Rachel Pauley: You've been an amazing recipe tester and assistant as well as a wonderful new friend. You have a great future ahead of you.

My cousin Erika and my dear family friend Tola: Thank you for your hours of cooking assistance.

Erica Breuer and Ashley Schuering: You are quite the amazing writers and perfectly captured my voice! Thank you both for helping me put my thoughts onto the page.

Johanna Voss: Thank you for managing my blog business and keeping me organized while I dove into this book.

Renegade Floral: Thank you for the beautiful tablescape arrangements.

Latina graphic artist, Zaida Diaz, creator of pwrgirlz.com, for designing altar graphic.

Dayra C. Testa @ayrelalove for the beautiful beaded jewelry and assistance with wardrobe styling.

Thank you to all the Mexican shops who dressed up these photos with artisanal home décor, textiles, clothing, flavors of Mexico, and fiesta supplies: nativashop.com, originmexico.com, verostiendita.com, artelexia.com, mexicoinmypocket.com, hernanmexico.com, mesachicparties.com, shopjavier.com, zinniafolkarts.com, and Sugar Skull Company (etsy.com/shop/SugarSkullCompany).

INDEX

A

Agua de Tamarindo, 177
Añejo-style tequila, 179
Apricot preserves
    Mini Cheese Empanadas with
        Apricot-Jalapeño Jam, 78–79
    Pavo Enchilado, 234–35
Arroz Blanco Mexicano, 275
Atole de Fresa, 216
Atole de Vainilla, 216
Avocados
    Avocado Tomatillo Salsa, 168
    Guacamole with
        Pomegranate, 98
    Ranchero Burgers, 152

B

Bacon
    Chorizo and Bacon Stuffing,
        232–33
    Ranchero Burgers, 152
Baileys Irish Cream
    Café de Olla with Irish
        Liqueur, 63
    Mexican Chocolate Martini, 45
Baked Churros with Lavender-
    Lemon Buttercream, 102–3
Barbacoa de Borrego, 69
Beans
    Huevos Rancheros, 115
    Sopaipillas Stuffed with Beef and
        Beans, 135–36
    Spinach and Bean Tacos, 18–19
Beef
    Chile Colorado con Carne y
        Papas, 186
    Chiles en Nogada, 171–73

Corned Beef Brisket Tacos, 54
Flautas de Carne Deshebrada a
    la Bandera, 168–70
Gorditas de Picadillo, 112–14
Machaca con Huevo, 129
Mexican Beef and Guinness
    Stew, 53
Ranchero Burgers, 152
Slow-Cooker Pot Roast, 188
Sopaipillas Stuffed with Beef and
    Beans, 135–36
Steak Fajitas, 154
Tampiqueña Steak, 116
Tequila and Lime Carne
    Asada, 91
Beer and stout
    Beer-Battered Shrimp Tacos, 14
    Beer Brats with Onions,
        Peppers, and Roasted Green
        Chile, 151
    Chelada, 140
    Mexican Beef and Guinness
        Stew, 53
    Mexican Beer Queso Dip, 147
    Mexican Chocolate Stout Cake
        with Irish Whiskey
        Ganache, 61–62
    Michelada with Clamato, 140
Beets
    Ensalada de Nochebuena, 245
Berries
    Atole de Fresa, 216
    Heart-Shaped Berry
        Empanadas, 36–38
    Mango and Strawberry
        Galette, 76–77
    Poinsettia Punch, 257
    Strawberry and Pistachio
        Paletas, 174

Birria, Lamb, 95–97
Biscochos, Orange, 248–49
Blanco-style tequila, 179
Bloody María with Serrano-Infused
    Tequila, 83
Bolillos, 226–27
Bourbon Sauce, Tres Leches Bread
    Pudding with, 26–27
Brats, Beer, with Onions, Peppers,
    and Roasted Green Chile, 151
Breads
    Bolillos, 226–27
    Caballeros Pobres, 111
    Chorizo and Bacon Stuffing,
        232–33
    Horchata & Mexican Chocolate
        Conchas, 217
    Irish Soda Bread with Roasted
        Green Chile, 58
    Pan de Muerto, 209–10
    Rosca de Navidad, 254–55
    Tres Leches Bread Pudding with
        Bourbon Sauce, 26–27
Brownies, Dulce de Leche, 41
Buñuelos with Gingerbread
    Piloncillo Syrup, 252–53
Burgers, Ranchero, 152

C

Caballeros Pobres, 111
Café de Olla with Irish Liqueur, 63
Cajeta Thumbprint Cookies, 39
Cakes
    Mexican Chocolate Stout Cake
        with Irish Whiskey
        Ganache, 61–62
    Mexican Coffee Cake, 118–19
Calabaza en Tacha, 189

Camotes Enmielados, 206
Carne Asada, Tequila and Lime, 91
Carnitas, Crispy Pork, 139
Carrots
    Arroz Blanco Mexicano, 275
    Mexican Beef and Guinness
        Stew, 53
    Slow-Cooker Pot Roast, 188
Cascarones, 84
Chacales, Sopa de, 17
Chantilly Cream, 42
Cheese
    Cheese Board, 35
    Chilaquiles Divorciadas, 12–13
    Elote, 156
    Ensalada de Coditos, 73
    Gringa al Pastor, 130–33
    Mar y Tierra Molcajete, 24
    Mexican Beer Queso Dip, 147
    Mini Cheese Empanadas with
        Apricot-Jalapeño Jam, 78–79
    Rajas con Queso, 230
    Ranchero Burgers, 152
    Red and Green Chile Cheese
        Enchiladas, 22–23
    Tampiqueña Steak, 116
    Walnut Sauce, 173
Chicken and Red Chile Tamales,
    260–63
Chilaquiles Divorciadas, 12–13
Chiles
    Beer Brats with Onions,
        Peppers, and Roasted Green
        Chile, 151
    Bloody María with Serrano-
        Infused Tequila, 83
    Chile Braised Pork Ribs, 205
    Chile Colorado con Carne y
        Papas, 186
    Chile Colorado Sauce, 69
    Chiles en Escabeche, 155
    Chiles en Nogada, 171–73
    Chipotle Cream Sauce, 14

Chipotle Mashed Sweet
    Potatoes, 229
Creamy Green Chile Sauce,
    22–23
Gringa al Pastor, 130–33
Hatch Chile Potato Salad, 148
Irish Soda Bread with Roasted
    Green Chile, 58
Jalapeño Mandarin
    Margarita, 101
Mexican Beer Queso Dip, 147
Mini Cheese Empanadas with
    Apricot-Jalapeño Jam, 78–79
Mole Rojo, 279
Pipián Verde, 57
Rajas con Queso, 230
Red Chile and Chicken Tamales,
    260–63
Red Chile Sauce, 13, 97
Salsa de Molcajete, 159
Spinach and Chile Verde
    Tortillas, 200–201
Tampiqueña Steak, 116
Chipotle Cream Sauce, 14
Chipotle Mashed Sweet
    Potatoes, 229
Chocolate
    Chocolate Mousse, 42
    Dulce de Leche Brownies, 41
    Mexican Chocolate Martini, 45
    Mexican Chocolate Stout Cake
        with Irish Whiskey
        Ganache, 61–62
    Mexican Hot Chocolate, 267
    Mole Rojo, 279
Chorizo and Bacon Stuffing,
    232–33
Christmas, 242
Christmas Ornaments, Tamal-
    Shaped, 268
Churros, Baked, with Lavender-
    Lemon Buttercream, 102–3
Cinco de Mayo, 88

Cinnamon
    Baked Churros with Lavender-
        Lemon Buttercream, 102–3
    Buñuelos with Gingerbread
        Piloncillo Syrup, 252–53
    Mexican Coffee Cake, 118–19
    Mexican Hot Chocolate, 267
    Orange Biscochos, 248–49
    Piloncillo Syrup, 252
Clamato, Michelada with, 140
Clothespin Cross, 28
Cochinita Pibil with Spicy Pickled
    Onions, 92–94
Coffee. See Café de Olla
Coffee Cake, Mexican, 118–19
Horchata & Mexican Chocolate
    Conchas, 217
Cookies
    Cajeta Thumbprint Cookies, 39
    Marranitos (Pig-Shaped
        Cookies), 214–15
    Mexican Sprinkle Cookies, 80
    Orange Biscochos, 248–49
    Polvorones, 280
    Red, White, and Green
        Polvorones, 250–51
    Witches' Fingers Sugar
        Cookies, 191
Corn
    Elote, 156
    Sopa de Verduras, 202
Corned Beef Brisket Tacos, 54
Corn husks (hojas)
    Red Chile and Chicken Tamales,
        260–63
    Sweet Raisin Tamales, 264–65
    Tamal-Shaped Christmas
        Ornaments, 268
Cranberries
    Poinsettia Punch, 257
Cream, Chantilly, 42
Crema
    Chipotle Cream Sauce, 14

Walnut Sauce, 173
Crème de cacao
    Mexican Chocolate Martini, 45
Crispy Pork Carnitas, 139
Cross, Clothespin, 28

D

Day of the Dead, 196
Day of the Dead altar, 199
Desserts
    Baked Churros with Lavender-
        Lemon Buttercream, 102–3
    Cajeta Thumbprint Cookies, 39
    Calabaza en Tacha, 189
    Camotes Enmielados, 206
    Chocolate Mousse, 42
    Dulce de Leche Brownies, 41
    Empanadas de Camote, 236–37
    Heart-Shaped Berry
        Empanadas, 36–38
    Mango and Strawberry
        Galette, 76–77
    Mexican Chocolate Stout Cake
        with Irish Whiskey
        Ganache, 61–62
    Mexican Sprinkle Cookies, 80
    Mini Cheese Empanadas with
        Apricot-Jalapeño Jam, 78–79
    Orange Biscochos, 248–49
    Polvorones, 280
    Red, White, and Green
        Polvorones, 250–51
    Strawberry and Pistachio
        Paletas, 174
    Sweet Raisin Tamales, 264–65
    Tres Leches Bread Pudding with
        Bourbon Sauce, 26–27
    Witches' Fingers Sugar
        Cookies, 191
Día de los Muertos, 196

Dips
    Guacamole with
        Pomegranate, 98
    Mexican Beer Queso Dip, 147
Drinks
    Agua de Tamarindo, 177
    Atole de Fresa, 216
    Atole de Vainilla, 216
    Blood Orange Marigold
        Margarita, 219
    Bloody María with Serrano-
        Infused Tequila, 83
    Café de Olla with Irish
        Liqueur, 63
    Chelada, 140
    El Ojo, 192
    Grilled Pineapple Smoked
        Mezcal, 137
    Guava Mimosas, 122
    Jalapeño Mandarin Margarita,
        101
    Mexican Chocolate Martini, 45
    Mexican Hot Chocolate, 267
    Mexican Sangria, 238
    Michelada with Clamato, 140
    Passion Fruit Margarita, 46
    Poinsettia Punch, 257
    Sandía con Agua Mineral, 160
    Watermelon-Pineapple Tequila
        Punch, 283
Dulce de Leche Brownies, 41
Dulce de Leche Orange
    Liqueur, 77

E

Easter, 66
Eggs
    Chilaquiles Divorciadas, 12–13
    Ham and Sweet Potato Hash, 70
    Huevos Rancheros, 115
    Machaca con Huevo, 129
El Ojo, 192

Elote, 156
Empanadas
    Empanadas de Camote, 236–37
    Heart-Shaped Berry
        Empanadas, 36–38
    Mini Cheese Empanadas with
        Apricot-Jalapeño Jam, 78–79
Enchiladas, Red and Green Chile
    Cheese, 22–23
Ensalada de Coditos, 73
Ensalada de Nochebuena, 245

F

Fajitas, Steak, 154
Father's Day, 126
Fish. See Tilapia
Flautas de Carne Deshebrada a la
    Bandera, 168–70
Fourth of July, 144
French toast. See Caballeros
    Pobres
Fruit. See also specific fruits
    Cheese Board, 35
    Ensalada de Nochebuena, 245
    Fresh Fruit Cups with Chamoy
        and Tajín, 121
    Mexican Sangria, 238
    Spring Fruit Salad with Tajín, 74

G

Galette, Mango and
    Strawberry, 76–77
Gorditas de Picadillo, 112–14
Grilled Pineapple Smoked
    Mezcal, 137
Gringa al Pastor, 130–33
Guacamole with Pomegranate, 98
Guava
    Cheese Board, 35
    Guava Mimosas, 122

Guinness stout
    Mexican Beef and Guinness
        Stew, 53
    Mexican Chocolate Stout
        Cake with Irish Whiskey
        Ganache, 61–62

H

Halloween, 182
Ham
    Ensalada de Coditos, 73
    Ham and Sweet Potato Hash, 70
Hash, Ham and Sweet Potato, 70
Hatch Chile Potato Salad, 148
Heart-Shaped Berry
    Empanadas, 36–38
Hominy
    Turkey Pozole Verde, 246
Hot Chocolate, Mexican, 267
Huevos Rancheros, 115

I

Irish liqueur
    Café de Olla with Irish
        Liqueur, 63
    Mexican Chocolate Martini, 45
Irish Soda Bread with Roasted
    Green Chile, 58
Irish Whiskey Ganache, Mexican
    Chocolate Stout Cake
    with, 61–62

J

Jalapeño Mandarin Margarita, 101
Jicama
    Ensalada de Nochebuena, 245
    Fresh Fruit Cups with Chamoy
        and Tajín, 121
    Spring Fruit Salad with Tajín, 74

L

Lamb
    Barbacoa de Borrego, 69
    Lamb Birria, 95–97
Lemon-Lavender Buttercream,
    Baked Churros with, 102–3
Lent, 10
Lime
    Chelada, 140
    Jalapeño Mandarin
        Margarita, 101
    Lime Corn Tortilla Chips, 167
    Tequila and Lime Carne
        Asada, 91

M

Machaca con Huevo, 129
Mangos
    Fresh Fruit Cups with Chamoy
        and Tajín, 121
    Mango and Strawberry
        Galette, 76–77
    Spring Fruit Salad with Tajín, 74
Margaritas
    Blood Orange Marigold
        Margarita, 219
    Jalapeño Mandarin
        Margarita, 101
    Passion Fruit Margarita, 46
Marranitos (Pig-Shaped
    Cookies), 214–15
Martini, Mexican Chocolate, 45
Mar y Tierra Molcajete, 24
Masa
    Red Chile and Chicken
        Tamales, 260–63
    Sweet Raisin Tamales, 264–65
Masa harina
    Atole de Fresa, 216
    Atole de Vainilla, 216

Gorditas de Picadillo, 112–14
    Spinach and Chile Verde
        Tortillas, 200–201
Meat. See Beef; Lamb; Pork
Mexican Beef and Guinness
    Stew, 53
Mexican Chocolate Martini, 45
Mexican Chocolate Stout Cake
    with Irish Whiskey
    Ganache, 61–62
Mexican Coffee Cake, 118–19
Mexican Hot Chocolate, 267
Mexican Independence Day, 164
Mexican lager
    Chelada, 140
    Mexican Beer Queso Dip, 147
    Michelada with Clamato, 140
Mexican Sangria, 238
Mexican Sprinkle Cookies, 80
Mezcal, Grilled Pineapple
    Smoked, 137
Michelada with Clamato, 140
Mimosas, Guava, 122
Mini Cheese Empanadas with
    Apricot-Jalapeño Jam, 78–79
Mini Piñatas, 104
Mole Rojo, 279
Mother's Day, 108
Mousse, Chocolate, 42
Mushrooms
    Mar y Tierra Molcajete, 24

N

Nopales
    Mar y Tierra Molcajete, 24
Nuts
    Mexican Coffee Cake, 118–19
    Mole Rojo, 279
    Polvorones, 280
    Strawberry and Pistachio
        Paletas, 174
    Walnut Sauce, 173

O

Olives
  Ensalada de Coditos, 73
  Veracruz-Style Tilapia, 21
Onions
  Beer Brats with Onions,
    Peppers, and Roasted Green
    Chile, 151
  Cochinita Pibil with Spicy Pickled
    Onions, 92–94
  Steak Fajitas, 154
  Tampiqueña Steak, 116
Orange liqueur
  Dulce de Leche Orange
    Liqueur, 77
  Jalapeño Mandarin
    Margarita, 101
  Mexican Sangria, 238
  Orange Biscochos, 248–49
  Poinsettia Punch, 257
  Watermelon-Pineapple Tequila
    Punch, 283
Oranges
  Blood Orange Marigold
    Margarita, 219
  Chipotle Mashed Sweet
    Potatoes, 229
  Ensalada de Nochebuena, 245
  Jalapeño Mandarin
    Margarita, 101
  Orange Biscochos, 248–49
  Pan de Muerto, 209–10
  Poinsettia Punch, 257

P

Paletas, Strawberry and
  Pistachio, 174
Pan de Muerto, 209–10
Papaya
  Fresh Fruit Cups with Chamoy
    and Tajín, 121

Spring Fruit Salad with Tajín, 74
Papel Picado, 104
Passion Fruit Margarita, 46
Pasta
  Ensalada de Coditos, 73
  Sopa de Letras, 276
Pavo Enchilado, 234–35
Peanuts
  Mole Rojo, 279
Pecans
  Polvorones, 280
Pepitas
  Pipián Verde, 57
  Salsa Verde, 246
  Spicy Roasted Pepitas, 185
  Witches' Fingers Sugar
    Cookies, 191
Peppers. *See also* Chiles
  Beer Brats with Onions,
    Peppers, and Roasted Green
    Chile, 151
  Mar y Tierra Molcajete, 24
  Roasted Peppers, 284
  Steak Fajitas, 154
Piloncillo Syrup, 252
Piñatas, Mini, 104
Pineapple
  Fresh Fruit Cups with Chamoy
    and Tajín, 121
  Grilled Pineapple Smoked
    Mezcal, 137
  Gringa al Pastor, 130–33
  Spring Fruit Salad with Tajín, 74
  Watermelon-Pineapple Tequila
    Punch, 283
Pipián Verde, 57
Pistachio and Strawberry
  Paletas, 174
Poinsettia Punch, 257
Polvorones
  Polvorones, 280
  Red, White, and Green
    Polvorones, 250–51

Pomegranate
  Ensalada de Nochebuena, 245
  Guacamole with
    Pomegranate, 98
Pork. *See also* Bacon; Ham
  Beer Brats with Onions,
    Peppers, and Roasted Green
    Chile, 151
  Chile Braised Pork Ribs, 205
  Chiles en Nogada, 171–73
  Chorizo and Bacon
    Stuffing, 232–33
  Cochinita Pibil with Spicy Pickled
    Onions, 92–94
  Crispy Pork Carnitas, 139
  Ensalada de Coditos, 73
  Gringa al Pastor, 130–33
Potatoes. *See also* Sweet potatoes
  Chile Colorado con Carne y
    Papas, 186
  Gorditas de Picadillo, 112–14
  Hatch Chile Potato Salad, 148
  Mexican Beef and Guinness
    Stew, 53
  Slow-Cooker Pot Roast, 188
Poultry. *See* Chicken; Turkey
Pozole Verde, Turkey, 246
Prickly pear
  Ensalada de Nochebuena, 245
Pudding, Tres Leches Bread, with
  Bourbon Sauce, 26–27
Pumpkin. *See* Calabaza
Punch
  Poinsettia Punch, 257
  Watermelon-Pineapple Tequila
    Punch, 283

R

Raisins
  Caballeros Pobres, 111
  Chiles en Nogada, 171–73
  Sweet Raisin Tamales, 264–65

Tres Leches Bread Pudding with
    Bourbon Sauce, 26–27
Rajas con Queso, 230
Ranchero Burgers, 152
Red, White, and Green
    Polvorones, 250–51
Red and Green Chile Cheese
    Enchiladas, 22–23
Red Chile and Chicken
    Tamales, 260–63
Red Chile Sauce, 13, 97
Reposado-style tequila, 179
Rice. *See* Arroz Blanco
Roasted Tomatillo Salsa, 13
Rolls. *See* Bolillos
Rosca de Navidad, 254–55

S

Saint Patrick's Day, 50
Salads
    Ensalada de Coditos, 73
    Ensalada de Nochebuena, 245
    Hatch Chile Potato Salad, 148
    Spring Fruit Salad with Tajín, 74
Salsas
    Avocado Tomatillo Salsa, 168
    Roasted Tomatillo Salsa, 13
    Salsa de Molcajete, 159
    Salsa Verde, 246
Sandía con Agua Mineral, 160
Sandwiches
    Beer Brats with Onions,
        Peppers, and Roasted Green
        Chile, 151
    Gringa al Pastor, 130–33
    Torta and Taco Bar with
        Thanksgiving Leftovers, 239
Sangria, Mexican, 238
Sauces
    Chile Colorado Sauce, 69
    Chipotle Cream Sauce, 14

Creamy Green Chile
    Sauce, 22–23
Dulce de Leche Orange
    Liqueur, 77
Mole Rojo, 279
Pipián Verde, 57
Rajas con Queso, 230
Red Chile Sauce, 13, 97
Walnut Sauce, 173
Sausage
    Beer Brats with Onions,
        Peppers, and Roasted Green
        Chile, 151
    Chorizo and Bacon
        Stuffing, 232–33
Seafood. *See* Shrimp; Tilapia
Shrimp
    Beer-Battered Shrimp Tacos, 14
    Mar y Tierra Molcajete, 24
Skulls, Sugar, 220
Slow-Cooker Pot Roast, 188
Soda Bread, Irish, with Roasted
    Green Chile, 58
Sopa de Chacales, 17
Sopa de Letras, 276
Sopa de Verduras, 202
Sopaipillas Stuffed with Beef and
    Beans, 135–36
Soups
    Sopa de Chacales, 17
    Sopa de Letras, 276
    Sopa de Verduras, 202
    Turkey Pozole Verde, 246
Spam
    Ensalada de Coditos, 73
Spicy Roasted Pepitas, 185
Spinach
    Spinach and Bean Tacos, 18–19
    Spinach and Chile Verde
        Tortillas, 200–201
Spring Fruit Salad with Tajín, 74
Sprinkle Cookies, Mexican, 80

Squash
    Calabaza en Tacha, 189
    Sopa de Verduras, 202
Stews
    Chile Colorado con Carne y
        Papas, 186
    Lamb Birria, 95–97
    Mexican Beef and Guinness
        Stew, 53
Strawberries
    Atole de Fresa, 216
    Mango and Strawberry
        Galette, 76–77
    Strawberry and Pistachio
        Paletas, 174
Stuffing, Chorizo and
    Bacon, 232–33
Sugar Skulls, 220
Sweet potatoes
    Camotes Enmielados, 206
    Chipotle Mashed Sweet
        Potatoes, 229
    Empanadas de Camote, 236–37
    Ham and Sweet Potato Hash, 70
Sweet Raisin Tamales, 264–65
Syrup, Piloncillo, 252

T

Tacos
    Beer-Battered Shrimp Tacos, 14
    Corned Beef Brisket Tacos, 54
    Lamb Birria, 95–97
    Spinach and Bean Tacos, 18–19
    Torta and Taco Bar with
        Thanksgiving Leftovers, 239
Tajín
    Fresh Fruit Cups with Chamoy
        and Tajín, 121
    Spring Fruit Salad with Tajín, 74
Tamalada, 258–59

Tamales
    Red Chile and Chicken
        Tamales, 260–63
    Sweet Raisin Tamales, 264–65
Tamal-Shaped Christmas
    Ornaments, 268
Tamarindo, Agua de, 177
Tampiqueña Steak, 116
Tequila
    añejo, 179
    blanco, 179
    Blood Orange Marigold
        Margarita, 219
    Bloody María with Serrano-
        Infused Tequila, 83
    El Ojo, 192
    Jalapeño Mandarin
        Margarita, 101
    Passion Fruit Margarita, 46
    reposado, 179
    tasting party, 178–79
    Tequila and Lime Carne
        Asada, 91
    Watermelon-Pineapple Tequila
        Punch, 283
Thanksgiving, 224
Tilapia, Veracruz-Style, 21
Tomatillos
    Avocado Tomatillo Salsa, 168
    Chile Colorado Sauce, 69
    Mole Rojo, 279
    Pipián Verde, 57
    Roasted Tomatillo Salsa, 13
    Salsa Verde, 246
Tomatoes
    Chile Colorado Sauce, 69
    Flautas de Carne Deshebrada a
        la Bandera, 168–70
    Salsa de Molcajete, 159
    Sopa de Letras, 276
    Veracruz-Style Tilapia, 21
Tomato juice

Bloody María with Serrano-
    Infused Tequila, 83
    Michelada with Clamato, 140
Torta and Taco Bar with
    Thanksgiving Leftovers, 239
Tortillas
    Beer-Battered Shrimp Tacos, 14
    Chilaquiles Divorciadas, 12–13
    Cochinita Pibil with Spicy Pickled
        Onions, 92–94
    Corned Beef Brisket Tacos, 54
    Crispy Pork Carnitas, 139
    Flautas de Carne Deshebrada a
        la Bandera, 168–70
    Gringa al Pastor, 130–33
    Huevos Rancheros, 115
    Lamb Birria, 95–97
    Lime Corn Tortilla Chips, 167
    Mar y Tierra Molcajete, 24
    Red and Green Chile Cheese
        Enchiladas, 22–23
    Spinach and Bean Tacos, 18–19
    Spinach and Chile Verde
        Tortillas, 200–201
    Steak Fajitas, 154
Tres Leches Bread Pudding with
    Bourbon Sauce, 26–27
Turkey
    Pavo Enchilado, 234–35
    Torta and Taco Bar with
        Thanksgiving Leftovers, 239
    Turkey Pozole Verde, 246

V

Vainilla, Atole de, 216
Valentine's Day, 32
Vegetables. See specific vegetables
Veracruz-Style Tilapia, 21
Vodka
    Mexican Chocolate Martini, 45

W

Walnuts
    Mexican Coffee Cake, 118–19
    Walnut Sauce, 173
Watermelon
    Fresh Fruit Cups with Chamoy
        and Tajín, 121
    Sandía con Agua Mineral, 160
    Spring Fruit Salad with Tajín, 74
    Watermelon-Pineapple Tequila
        Punch, 283
Wine
    Guava Mimosas, 122
    Mexican Sangria, 238
    Poinsettia Punch, 257
Witches' Fingers Sugar
    Cookies, 191

weldon**owen**

an imprint of Insight Editions
P.O. Box 3088
San Rafael, CA 94912
www.weldonowen.com

CEO Raoul Goff
VP Publisher Roger Shaw
Associate Publisher Amy Marr
Editorial Director Katie Killebrew
Assistant Editor Jourdan Plautz
VP Creative Chrissy Kwasnik
VP Manufacturing Alix Nicholaeff
Sr Production Manager Joshua Smith
Sr Production Manager, Subsidiary Rights Lina s Palma-Temena

Design by Ashley Quackenbush and Rita Sowins. Case design by Megan Sinead Harris.

Weldon Owen would also like to thank Sharon Silva.

ISBN: 978-1-68188-917-7

ROOTS of PEACE   REPLANTED PAPER

Insight Editions, in association with Roots of Peace, will plant two trees for each tree used in the manufacturing of this book. Roots of Peace is an internationally renowned humanitarian organization dedicated to eradicating land mines worldwide and converting war-torn lands into productive farms and wildlife habitats. Roots of Peace will plant two million fruit and nut trees in Afghanistan and provide farmers there with the skills and support necessary for sustainable land use.

Manufactured in China by Insight Editions
10 9 8 7 6 5 4 3 2 1